T0079853

TOMATO

Edible

Series Editor: Andrew F. Smith

EDIBLE is a revolutionary series of books dedicated to food and drink that explores the rich history of cuisine. Each book reveals the global history and culture of one type of food or beverage.

Already published

Apple Erika Janik · *Banana* Lorna Piatti-Farnell
Barbecue Jonathan Deutsch and Megan J. Elias · *Beef* Lorna Piatti-Farnell
Beer Gavin D. Smith · *Berries* Heather Arndt Anderson
Biscuits and Cookies Anastasia Edwards · *Brandy* Becky Sue Epstein
Bread William Rubel · *Cabbage* Meg Muckenhoupt · *Cake* Nicola Humble
Caviar Nichola Fletcher · *Champagne* Becky Sue Epstein
Cheese Andrew Dalby · *Chillies* Heather Arndt Anderson
Chocolate Sarah Moss and Alexander Badenoch
Cocktails Joseph M. Carlin · *Coffee* Jonathan Morris
Corn Michael Owen Jones · *Curry* Colleen Taylor Sen
Dates Nawal Nasrallah · *Doughnut* Heather Delancey Hunwick
Dumplings Barbara Gallani · *Edible Flowers* Constance L. Kirker
and Mary Newman · *Eggs* Diane Toops · *Fats* Michelle Phillipov
Figs David C. Sutton · *Game* Paula Young Lee
Gin Lesley Jacobs Solmonson · *Hamburger* Andrew F. Smith
Herbs Gary Allen · *Herring* Kathy Hunt · *Honey* Lucy M. Long
Hot Dog Bruce Kraig · *Ice Cream* Laura B. Weiss · *Lamb* Brian Yarvin
Lemon Toby Sonneman · *Lobster* Elisabeth Townsend
Melon Sylvia Lovegren · *Milk* Hannah Velten · *Moonshine* Kevin R. Kosar
Mushroom Cynthia D. Bertelsen · *Nuts* Ken Albala · *Offal* Nina Edwards
Olive Fabrizia Lanza · *Onions and Garlic* Martha Jay
Oranges Clarissa Hyman · *Oyster* Carolyn Tillie · *Pancake* Ken Albala
Pasta and Noodles Kantha Shelke · *Pickles* Jan Davison · *Pie* Janet Clarkson
Pineapple Kaori O'Connor · *Pizza* Carol Helstosky
Pomegranate Damien Stone · *Pork* Katharine M. Rogers
Potato Andrew F. Smith · *Pudding* Jeri Quinzio · *Rice* Renee Marton
Rum Richard Foss · *Salad* Judith Weinraub · *Salmon* Nicolaas Mink
Sandwich Bee Wilson · *Sauces* Maryann Tebben · *Sausage* Gary Allen
Seaweed Kaori O'Connor · *Shrimp* Yvette Florio Lane
Soup Janet Clarkson · *Spices* Fred Czarra · *Sugar* Andrew F. Smith
Sweets and Candy Laura Mason · *Tea* Helen Saberi · *Tequila* Ian Williams
Tomato Clarissa Hyman · *Truffle* Zachary Nowak · *Vodka* Patricia Herlihy
Water Ian MilleR · *Whiskey* Kevin R. Kosar · *Wine* Marc Millon

Tomato

A Global History

Clarissa Hyman

REAKTION BOOKS

Published by Reaktion Books Ltd
Unit 32, Waterside
44–48 Wharf Road
London N1 7UX, UK
www.reaktionbooks.co.uk

First published 2019

Copyright © Clarissa Hyman 2019

All rights reserved
No part of this publication may be reproduced, stored in a retrieval
system, or transmitted, in any form or by any means, electronic,
mechanical, photocopying, recording or otherwise, without the prior
permission of the publishers

Printed and bound in China by 1010 Printing International Ltd

A catalogue record for this book is available from the British Library

ISBN 978 1 78914 083 5

Recipe for 'Tomates à la Lucie' (p. 134) from Joseph Delteil,
La Cuisine paléolithique (Éditions de Paris: Paris, 2017)
reproduced by kind permission of Les Éditions de Paris.

Contents

Introduction

At first sight there may seem little to connect the Chilean poet Pablo Neruda and the American country singer-songwriter John Denver, but they both have devoted verses to the tomato. In 'Ode to Tomatoes', the former takes pleasure in the quotidian and describes how the union of the tomato with onion, oil, pepper and salt offers a 'gift/ of fiery colour/ and cool completeness', while Denver sagely sings about two things whose value is beyond measure, love and home-grown tomatoes.

Yet, the tomato is anything but commonplace. The tomato world is a rainbow nation of shapes, colours, textures and sizes, from luscious, curvaceous and ribbed forms to clusters of tight little cherries, tart and cheery green toms and elongated 'plums'. They range from the perfectly round (globe) to the highly flattened (oblate); they can be oval or egg-shaped, long and slender, segmented, heart or pear-shaped. They can be as small as a pea or as large as a grapefruit: imagine, if you will, a mouse next to an elephant.

There is a tomato for every time, place or use. Cherry, grape and cocktail tomatoes have conquered the snacking world; the large beefsteak has nothing to do with flavour and everything to do with texture and density. Tomatoes can be

7

Sliced tomato cross-sections.

juicy or dry, soft or succulent, and the balance between acid and sweet, fullness and blandness, complexity and simplicity is the benchmark of a good tomato, as is the dominance of juice over water. Today there is a multitude of choice also in terms of colour and markings: pale orange, pink, yellow with red swirls or stripes, red with gold zigzags, green, brown, black and white. Colour is not always a guide to taste, and there are as many exceptions as there are general rules when it comes to matching flavour and hues. Every tomato lover has their personal palate.

It is hard to imagine a world without tomatoes. Both landscape and cuisine have been changed by the eye-catching neon-red vegetable-cum-fruit on its tangled green vine. In the kitchen it has an essential role and pervades every part of our food experience. In Romagna, Italy, a nosy person is sometimes named Don Pomodoro because, like the tomato, they are into everything. And now they are everywhere.

A colourful variety of tomatoes in Borough Market, London.

Five new varieties of tomato, from a Childs catalogue of 1920.

The unusually coloured Indigo Rose tomato, a blue tomato cultivar.

The tomato is arguably the most widely grown 'vegetable' in the world, cultivated as far north as Iceland and as far south as the Falkland Islands. Tomato seedlings have even been grown in space, circling the Earth by satellite. However, the plant's very ubiquity has given us both the best and worst of horticultural practice, encompassing both global big business and the noble heritage-seed saver.

Transformation is an essential part of the tomato's journey from obscure wild plant to everyday shelf-filler, from exotic to mundane, from supposedly poisonous and aphrodisiac to nutritious and desirable. Centuries of domestication and efforts by growers and gardeners have defined the story of how the tomato emerged from the margins of horticulture to be cultivated on a mass scale and consumed universally.

Every link in the chain to produce the ripened fruit has been the focus of intense intervention and innovation: 'seed manufacture, energy, atmosphere, pollination, nutrient

A field of tomato plants.

provision, pest control, grading, packaging, distribution, information technology, consumption'.[1] The distinction between fresh and processed tomato commodities led to a fundamental division: the realm of the latter consists of hundreds of thousands of farm and factory workers, then of thousands of tomato farms, thousands of processing tomato factories, hundreds of specialist processing tomato companies, a dozen key transnational corporations, tens of thousands of individual products, brand names, trademarks and patents, and millions of consumers.[2] The mainstream model for fresh tomatoes is similar, if smaller in scale. Nonetheless there is

La Tomatina festival, held annually in Buñol in Valencia, Spain.

The global tomato: an art exhibition in Hong Kong, 2012.

an inherent irony, as the authors of *Exploring the Tomato* note, in that the contemporary global tomato is both natural and artificial in that nothing is 'left to nature'.[3]

The growth of alternatives, such as farmers' markets and heritage varieties, to the agro-industrialized, corporate tomato and convenience-based food chains, however, shows a persistent and dynamic desire for a diverse tomato culture that will give us a wholesome and exuberant taste of history. We still yearn for a 'human tomato'.

You say tomato, and I say *Solanum lycopersicum*.

I
Origins

Tomatoes are ubiquitous in the modern world but their fleshy, shiny proliferation could hardly have been foreseen when the original fruits, some no bigger than redcurrants, first grew in northwestern South America. The progeny of these vines were irregular and erratic in habit but they were the founding fathers of what has been described as 'the human tomato', in the sense that they have grown up entwined with the global history of food.[1]

Botanical classification has evolved over the centuries but the tomato is now accepted as part of the Solanaceae family, a highly diverse group of flowering plants that also includes the potato, aubergine (eggplant), tobacco, deadly nightshade and petunia. *Solanum* is the largest genus, and Linnaeus placed the tomato within this category in 1753, calling it *Solanum lycopersicum* (which derives from the Greek for wolf peach). However, the botanist Philip Miller later gave the tomato its own genus, *Lycopersicon esculentum* (the latter simply means edible), thereby sowing the seeds of considerable taxonomic confusion in the process.

However, genetic evidence, based on molecular studies by David Spooner in the early 1990s, established that Miller's *Lycopersicon* is 'nested' within *Solanum* and, as a result, its species

Solanum pimpinellifolium, the currant tomato.

transferred to the latter as a sub-genus. So Linnaeus appears to have got it right after all, although *L. esculentum* continues to have its adherents. The taxonomic debate continues but you may as well quarrel over the correct pronunciation of the rosy-red objects in question and, like Mr Gershwin, make your choice and just call the whole thing off.

Many wild species have been identified: most are green-fruited, although a few are coloured, and are found in habitats ranging from the deserts of the Pacific coast to the green valleys and damp mountains of the Andes, as well as the Galápagos islands. They can thrive in extremely harsh conditions, often surviving with little water as long as they are not killed outright by frost or have waterlogged roots. Most, however, have very small populations, making them vulnerable to extinction. The indigenous Peruvian chronicler Guamán Poma mentions the occasional eating of wild tomato fruit in the Inca empire, but other references are rare. Although the wild fruits are not toxic, their complex taste, according to legendary tomato geneticist Charles Rick, is for the most part extremely unpalatable.[2]

One of the main wild species and distant ancestor of the modern tomato is *Solanum pimpinellifolium*, the currant tomato. The plant has a bushy growth and sprays of tiny flame-red berries that split when ripe to release minute seeds. It is an aggressive colonizer that grows like a weed from northern Chile to Peru-Ecuador. Another wild tomato, *Solanum cerasiforme* or cherry tomato, is thought to have originated out of the former although demarcations between them are not straightforward. The cherry is also the only wild tomato found outside South America and bears greater genetic resemblance to the cultivated tomato than to other wild

Tomatillos are still much used in Mexican cooking but are unrelated to the tomato.

Varieties of *Solanum cerasiforme*, cherry tomatoes.

species. Recent investigations, however, suggest that it is a mixture of wild and cultivated tomatoes rather than being 'ancestral' to the latter.[3]

Although the detailed parentage of the modern tomato remains somewhat unclear, ethnobotanists and geneticists have attempted to track down the geographical centre of domestication. It is thought that a type of pre-domestication took place in the Andean region before the process continued in Mesoamerica, where seeds and plants were carried northwards on the wind as weeds or by birds, wildlife and indigenous peoples. Rachel Laudan describes how beans, squash, tomatoes and chillies were planted in Olmec villages in small forest clearings surrounded by cacao bushes and avocado trees.[4] And Andrew F. Smith notes how genetic mutation around this time likely produced a larger, lumpier, multi-celled fruit.[5]

Much later, in the Puebla-Veracruz area of Mexico, the most significant wave of domestication occurred under the Aztecs. They adopted the plant easily, most likely because of its general similarity to the abundant tomatillo (husk tomato) or *Physalis philadelphica*, which was already a familiar native food. The latter, both wild and cultivated, was commonly used in sauces and salsas: in the view of the botanist J. A. Jenkins, it was 'undoubtedly the original tomato of the Aztecs and related peoples'.[6] The tomato was not of great importance, simply an extra plant in the maize fields. However, compared to the tomatillo it had a greater resistance to rot, plus a particularly colourful appearance, and in the end the tomatillo became marginalized, an also-ran in the race to conquer the way the world eats.

The word 'tomato' derives from the Nahuatl *tomatl*, a generic term for a globose fruit or berry with seeds and watery flesh sometimes enclosed in a membrane. It was also described by the Franciscan friar and priest Alonso de Molina in his Nahuatl–Spanish dictionary (1571) as referring to 'a certain fruit used to add a sour flavour to stews and sauces'. As many nouns in Nahuatl that ended in 'tl' were absorbed into Spanish, their suffix was replaced with 'e'. Hence *tomatl* became the Spanish *tomate*.

Counter-intuitively, at least to European minds, the green and tart tomatillo with its papery husk is called *tomate* in certain parts of Mexico; the word for the (mostly) red tomato is *xitomatl* or *jitomate*, meaning peeled or skinned tomato. Unfortunately, some of the sixteenth-century chroniclers of native life made no distinction between *tomate* and *xitomatl* or *jitomate*, a point that was to become a source of future uncertainty.

From Bernardino de Sahagún's *The General History of the Things of New Spain*, written in both Nahuatl and Spanish within a decade of the Conquest, it is evident that both fruits were on display in the local markets. Sometimes described as the world's first anthropologist, the Franciscan friar documented many aspects of Aztec life and he vividly and meticulously noted three types of red tomato and seven types of tomatillo, although it is not quite clear to which he was referring when he described, almost in the form of a prose poem,

> large tomatoes, small tomatoes, green tomatoes, leaf tomatoes, thin tomatoes, sweet tomatoes, large serpent tomatoes, nipple-shaped tomatoes, coyote tomatoes, sand tomatoes, and those which are yellow, very yellow, quite yellow, red, very red, quite ruddy, bright red, reddish, rosy dawn coloured . . .[7]

He also came across the 'bad tomato seller' who sold 'spoiled tomatoes, bruised tomatoes, and those which cause diarrhoea'. Tomatoes, he noted, featured in chicken and shrimp casseroles, even with tortillas from street sellers. The scene is remarkably immediate:

> He sells foods, sauces, hot sauces; fried, *olla*-cooked, juices, sauces of juices, shredded with chile, with squash

seeds, with tomatoes, with smoked chile, with hot chile, with yellow chile, with mild red chile sauce, with 'bird excrement' sauce . . . He sells toasted beans, cooked beans, mushroom sauce, sauce of small squash, sauce of large tomatoes, sauce of ordinary tomatoes, sauce of various kinds of sour herbs, avocado sauce . . .[8]

Some years later, José de Acosta, a sixteenth-century Jesuit missionary and naturalist, reported the sight of what clearly were red tomatoes, according to Janet Long, when he described them as fresh and healthy, large and juicy, and said they made a tasty sauce and were even good to eat on their own.[9]

The cultivated tomato or 'plump thing with a navel' was first scientifically catalogued by Francisco Hernández, a naturalist and personal physician to Philip II. He gave only a brief nod to the red tomato and was more interested in the tomatillo, to which he devoted five pages listing the different types and their culinary and medicinal uses. His observations, however, are undermined by the fact that his chapter on tomatoes is illustrated with a drawing of a tomatillo.[10]

Francisco Cervantes de Salazar, rector of the newly founded University of Mexico, described in 1544 how tomatoes were added to sauces and stews along with ground squash seeds to offset the bite of chillies while adding a pleasing tartness. Less appetizingly, in 1632 Bernal Díaz del Castillo recounted that when the Spanish went across the country from Veracruz to Tenochtitlan, the natives wanted to 'kill and eat us and eat our meat' and had pots ready with chillies, tomatoes and salt. He also mentioned that the Aztecs ate the arms and legs of their sacrificial victims with a sauce made with chilli peppers, tomatoes, wild onions and salt. As Janet Long points out, the ingredients were nearly the same as that of *salsa mexicana*, used in most Mexican homes today.[11]

Mexican tomato salsa being made in a *molcajete*, a stone mortar.

The mega-tough Spanish explorers of the day may have been fearsome warriors and adventurers, buccaneering and bloodthirsty, but they were cautious and conservative when it came to new foods. They likely would have tried to shape the exotic and unknown into a safe, familiar European scheme: get it wrong and they could be poisoned. Their wariness was both a result of their unwillingness to try new things, a reluctance to eat the food of irreligious natives and a question of survival. Manioc, for example, made the Spanish extremely sick before they understood it had to be peeled before serving. The tomato would initially have seemed an enigma, resembling a fruit but too acidic to be used as one.

Foot soldiers of the Spanish armies may have been reluctant to try the local food but it was a different story in the palaces, convents, townhouses and haciendas of the wealthy and powerful. As Rachel Laudan argues, 'In spite of the European disdain for the cuisine of Mesoamerica, intermarriage and servants meant that the kitchens of the conquerors and the conquered could not be kept completely separate.' She describes an interesting, fusion-style, eighteenth-century Catholic-*criollo* recipe: braised fowl *mestizo*, a 'mixed race' dish of hen with Mexican tomatoes and chillies.[12]

Rebecca Earle offers a slightly different take. She writes that most settlers found it difficult to avoid such foods altogether but those who embraced them too enthusiastically were viewed with some suspicion, such as those denounced for 'drifting about amongst the Indians eating chilli and tomatoes'.[13]

Nonetheless, once back home the conquistadores were keen to show off their spoils, from strange plants to precious spices and exotic animals, to the rulers who paid for their adventures – and it might not be out of the question that some returning Spaniards had developed a taste for *criollo* cooking. Not only were these ingredients and dishes introduced to Spain but they were deliberately spread throughout the Spanish- and Portuguese-speaking world, especially the Caribbean and the Philippines, then onwards to India, Turkey and the Ottoman Empire, entering Europe from the east as well as the west. Thanks to an army of invaders, explorers, missionaries and traders, the internationalization of the tomato had begun.

2
New World to Old World

By 1523 the Mexican conquest was complete and the country subdued. There was a regular timetable of ships travelling the 'silver route' between Veracruz and the principal Spanish port of Seville but just when or how the plants or seeds were transported remains hazy. It is most likely that they travelled in seed form, as plants probably would not have lasted the long sea voyage. They may have been carried on purpose by those Spaniards who had grown used to the flavours of the New World; others might have found their way on board accidentally in cargo or baggage.

Details will probably never be known, in part because of the plant's seeming lack of commercial importance, although the moderate Mediterranean climate provided a welcoming habitat. Many of these undocumented immigrants would have been planted in the fields, and eaten fresh, perhaps with a little salt, well before they were identified by botanical scholars.[1]

It was only in the seventeenth century that the tomato became widely cultivated in the gardens of the elite, as an exotic ornamental or medicinal curiosity given extra cachet by its New World origins. Tomatoes were, however, largely an unknown quantity when it came to kitchen use: too acidic to be eaten green, quickly spoiling once ripe and breaking up when cooked. Nor were they particularly attractive, with pallid flowers and strong-smelling leaves that were far more intense than today's varieties. Along with the chilli and potato, they were also regarded with suspicion as a result of their solanaceous family membership.

Gardener-priest Gregorio de los Ríos worked in the royal botanical gardens of Aranjuez. In 1592 he listed sixteen species growing there of New World origin, including tomatoes, which he described as 'pomates'.[2] He noted that they had ribbed sections that turned red and contained seeds, and that the plants lasted for two or three years and required a lot of water. He added that they were said to be good for sauces but did not admit to having tried them.[3]

An early mention of the tomato appears in the purchase book of the Hospital de la Sangre in Seville in 1608, although this may have been the first and last time the cooks of the religious order attempted to introduce the tomato into the daily diet, as it does not seem to have been recorded again.[4] On the 1659 registry of the House of Aguilar in Montilla, however, lunch menus included chicken with tomatoes and stewed tomatoes with hard-boiled eggs, and tomatoes frequently appeared on their shopping lists.[5] Nonetheless, there is a curious lack of reference to the tomato in the culinary and household works of the Spanish Golden Age, an apparent imbalance between its arrival and use.

Jeanne Allard suggests several reasons for this absence. First, cookbooks tend to be a summary of many years of practice. The royal chef, educated from a young age in court cuisine, would understand the tastes and preferences of his masters; it would be too risky to serve up a hitherto unknown foodstuff until it had been thoroughly tried and tested. Second, it is most unlikely that these newly introduced plants would

Matthäus Merian's 1638 map of Seville.

have had the gustatory qualities they have today (Salazar had commented, for example, that tomatoes tasted similar to sour grapes.) Additionally, vegetables and salad greens played a far smaller role than meat in the diet of the rich and were often considered unhealthy, especially if wild and uncultivated.[6] Francisco Núñez de Oria in late sixteenth-century Castile described people who ate salads and vegetables as having 'all the colours of the rainbow in their complexions and faces'.[7]

Finally, Allard says, with their growing accessibility tomatoes were no longer a status symbol. And, she notes, we should not be surprised the tomato figured so little in upperclass Spanish kitchens when, unlike turkey and chocolate, it was largely ignored by the elite of the newcomers in Mexico itself. If anyone was eating the tomato it was the peasant and lower classes (as well as the religious orders), especially in Andalusia, where the principal port for voyages to and from Mexico was, of course, Seville.[8]

According to Carolyn A. Nadeau, tomatoes were eaten in salads, both cold and warm, as well as in sauces throughout the seventeenth century, and indications of their popular use is found in poems, plays and paintings.[9] Janet Long notes that sixteenth- and seventeenth-century Spanish writers were fascinated with all things from the New World and delighted in borrowing vocabulary from Hispanic Indian languages.[10] In Lope de Vega's play *The Eighth Wonder* (1618), a character refers to the sweet pleasure of a tomato in season, and Agustín Moreto, a seventeenth-century Madrid-born playwright, mentions a *puchero* or stew served with a spicy tomato sauce in *El Entremés con Mariquita*.[11] Around the same period, in a play called *Love the Doctor* by Tirso de Molina, a racy line about tomato salads with rosy cheeks 'at times sweet, at times hot' aimed to whet the audience's appetite in every sense.[12]

The Angels' Kitchen, a 1646 painting by Murillo for the Franciscan convent of Seville, includes an unmistakable tomato lined up in a corner alongside squash and cherubs. Tomatoes

Luis Egidio Meléndez, *Still-life with Artichokes and Tomatoes in a Landscape*, early 1770s, oil on canvas.

also feature in other Spanish paintings of the seventeenth century, such as Juan van der Hamen's *Pomona and Vertumnus* and *Still-life with Fruit Bowl and Sweets*; Francisco Barrera's *The Month of July*; and various paintings by Luis Meléndez, such as *Still-life with Artichokes and Tomatoes in a Landscape*.[13]

Spain's glory years were to go into reverse in the late seventeenth century. Food became scarce as a result of the expulsion of the Moriscos – Muslims forcibly converted to Christianity – and consequent decline in agricultural production. Both famine and the return of the plague took their toll. There are a few references that indicate that tomatoes had become more incorporated into the diets of both rich and poor, out of preference for the former and necessity for the latter. Either way, tomatoes were here to stay and flourished throughout the country, especially in the south, where they could be harvested year-round and were often eaten for

Ribbed Spanish tomatoes.

Gazpacho, a cold Andalusian soup commonly made with tomatoes, peppers and other raw vegetables.

breakfast. A plate of fried red tomatoes and peppers may often have been the main meal of the day.[14]

As the Spanish empire crumbled, recipe writing was not, perhaps, a high priority, and there are few cookery books of the period. Two exceptions were the *Book of Notations on Stews and Sweets* (1740) by María Rosa Calvillo de Teruel, which featured tomatoes in over a dozen recipes,[15] and *The Art of Confectionery* (1747) by the royal pastry chef Juan de la Mata, which included two recipes for tomato sauce. Other written sources are equally scant: in the *Kitchen Account Book* of the College of Corpus Christi in Valencia, for example, it was recorded that on Saturday 14 January 1746, they had 'three cardoons, garlic, tomatoes and large peppers' for dinner, and in a later agricultural work, published in 1765 in Valencia, there is an extensive discussion of tomato-growing methods.[16]

Under the influence of a new merchant class, as the eighteenth century progressed, a growing emphasis was placed on

simple, regional food and local ingredients. Juan Altami
was a Spanish Franciscan friar who published *The New Ar*
Cookery in 1745. It was a short compendium of brightly
voured, healthy recipes for cooks of modest means in wh
tomatoes gave a lively twist to familiar recipes. Gradua
tomatoes were incorporated into traditional dishes such
gazpacho and salted cod.

Sometimes he would replace spices with tomato, garlic a
lemon, a small step that would in time greatly impact Span
cookery. He also used tomatoes as an acidic condime
instead of lime, orange or verjus. As Vicky Hayward po
ders, 'Quite why Altamiras innovated by using tomatoes
a seasoning rather than the main ingredient of a sauce
do not know, unless it was to spread the flavour of a limi
supply through as many dishes as possible.' Whatever t
reason, he was a particular enthusiast for the tomato, descr
ing its use in a braised lamb dish as so good 'you will fi
yourself licking your fingers – unless, of course, you ar
smooth-mannered man'.[17]

3
The Italian Tomato

Despite growing interest in the tomato, appreciation of fresh fruit and vegetables was more advanced on the Italian peninsula than in Spain. Population growth in the second half of the sixteenth century, exacerbated by periods of famine, was an incentive to experiment with the new foods from America, but even in Italy tomatoes were not easy to introduce into the mainstream: they looked curious, had a strange texture, and went from hard, acidic green to soft and squishy ripeness.[1]

Initially, botanists' interest in New World plants resulted from the hope of discovering miraculous pharmacological properties. Botanists recorded these in 'Herbals' illustrated with detailed woodcut engravings. The tomato's advance into the kitchen was aided by the skill of Italian gardeners who soon transformed the new arrival into a more tempting large, smooth fruit with a strong, thick skin.

In 1548 the trend-setting, horticulturally innovative Cosimo de' Medici received a basket of tomatoes at the court in Florence, sent from the family's Gallo estate, although it is unknown what sort they were or what he did with them.[2] Possibly he and his courtiers were simply happy to gaze upon them as they might an exotic art installation.

The sixteenth-century botanist Pietro Mattioli called them *malum aureum*, or golden apples, which suggests their main colour at the time. He wrote how they can be 'milled like pink apples or segmented into wedges of spring-green colour, and when mature, some plants are red like blood, while others are golden'. He also noted that 'some eat it fried in oil with salt and pepper like aubergine'. In other words, it was a fruit that was eaten like a vegetable. His contemporary Costanzo Felici described fruit of an intense yellow or vivid red, which were 'to my taste better to look at than to eat'.[3]

The Old World was indeed largely unappreciative; the jury was still out. For one thing the tomato belonged to the Solanaceae family, which included poisonous plants such as deadly nightshade, stinkweed, henbane and woody night-shade. To make matters worse, Mattioli erroneously referred to the tomato as a member of the mandrake family, the plant of black magic, witches, monstrosity and death as well as aphrodisiac powers. The mandrake was also known as *mala terrestia* or earth apple. It was not propitious, and the botanist's mistake was to be perpetuated down the centuries.

Another misleading link with love seems to have derived from the Flemish botanist Rembert Dodoens, writing around the same time as Mattioli. He gave the tomato the name *poma amoris*, which was adopted in translation by the French and English as *pomp d'amour* and love apple respectively. Public imagination did the rest. The love myth was especially prevalent in the seventeenth century: Hyacinthus Ambrosias noted that the love apple was so called 'because amatory powers are attributed to it or because it has a fitting elegance or beauty worthy to command love'.[4] Yet it makes little sense. As David Gentilcore notes, if anything, the supposed 'cold' properties of the tomato should actually lead to its use as a desire damp-ener rather than the opposite.[5] Andrew F. Smith emphasizes

Pierre-Auguste Renoir, *Courgettes, Tomatoes and Aubergines*, 1915, oil on canvas.

that there is little evidence that anyone in America or Britain ever considered the tomato to be an aphrodisiac.[6]

In time the tomato became known as *pomo d'oro*, or 'golden apple', and finally the Italian *pomodoro*. Apart from the lyricism, this example of Renaissance humanism established a continuity with classical antiquity in a reference to the fabled garden of the Hesperides.[7] Alternatively, as Rudolf Grewe suggested, the link with the aubergine, the *pomme des Mours* (fruit of the Moors), may have resulted in the cognate *pomme d'amour* and was thus another route to the Italian *pomodoro*.[8] Two nations not usually thought of as über-romantic, the Germans and British, kept the poetic name for many years: *Liebesapfel* and 'love apples'. In the end, however, some variant of the Nahuan *tomatl* replaced other names throughout the world.

One of the few who recommended tomatoes as good to eat was Federico Ceso, a seventeenth-century Roman aristocrat with an interest in botany who commissioned an illustrated herbal based on Hernández's work. Although a small number did eat them either out of greed, sensation-seeking or simple poverty, more typical is the report provided by Melchior Sebizius in 1650 in *On the Faculty of Food* when he wrote, 'they are so cold and moist they must be cooked with pepper, salt and oil but our cooks absolutely reject them, even though they grow easily and copiously in gardens.'[9]

Sephardic Jewish communities were an exception and during the Renaissance they flourished throughout Italy, especially in Livorno, where they were at the centre of trade networks that connected them to north African and southern Mediterranean communities. Tomatoes were commonly used, and a fried cod and tomato stew is one of the recipes of Jewish origin still popular today.[10] Probably Arabs, who were thrown out of Spain by the *reconquista*, also brought the tomato with them to the south of Italy.

John Ray, a British naturalist who travelled throughout Italy in the 1660s, noted how tomatoes were cooked with squash, pepper, salt and oil, a method that harked back to Hernández's descriptions of New Spain. He suggested, however, that they not be eaten but rubbed onto the skin to help cure scabies.[11]

Antonio Latini was steward to the Spanish court of Naples and in his ambitious two-volume household book *The Modern Steward* (1692–4) he included local products of the south, New World ingredients and more herbs than spices. He mentions an aubergine, squash and tomato soup, and gives the first printed recipe for a tomato sauce. It is described as *alla spagnuola* or 'in the Spanish style' and includes chillies. John Dickie, however, makes the somewhat dismissive point that when it came to the tomato, 'Latini was as oblivious to its potential as the rest of his contemporaries. He suggests perfunctorily that it makes a "very tasty sauce for boiled meat, or other things" and never mentions it again.'[12]

Antonio Latini of Collamato, illustration c. 1692.

Later recipes for tomato sauce dropped chillies as an ingredient, marking the separation of these two iconic items so associated with the cooking of Mesoamerica. Without the chilli, the tomato could then marry more easily with other European ingredients and integrate into traditional dishes. 'Apples of Love', reported the Quaker merchant Peter Collinson in 1742, 'are very much used in Italy to putt when ripe into their brooths and soups giving it a pretty tart taste.'[13]

Rapid kitchen assimilation was paralleled by horticultural acclimatization and dietary acculturation as the use of the fruit spread northwards and as new ideas prevailed in medical

Lycopersicon Galeni. Ang. 217. — 5.℞.H. 50. — Ital. *Pomidoro*. — gall. *Pomme d'amour*
Magdalena Bouchard sculpsit

Illustration of 'Lycopersicon galeni', from Giorgio Bonelli, *Hortus Romanus* (1772).

Illustration showing Joseph Reinach, a supporter of Alfred Dreyfus, being attacked with tomatoes. From *Le Petit Journal*, 15 July 1900.

and scientific spheres about the process of digestion. In 1759 Giovanni Targioni Tozzetti, a physician-botanist, included tomatoes among the 'fruits prized by men as foodstuffs or as condiments for them'.[14] Then, in 1773, Vincenzo Corrado published *The Gallant Cook*. He was a Benedictine monk who travelled throughout the Peninsula gathering recipes from different regions. These include tomatoes stuffed with veal or rice simmered in milk, butter, sugar and cinnamon; tomato, egg and ricotta croquettes; and a pungent-sounding tomato sauce made with vinegar, garlic and rue to accompany mutton. His recipe for tomatoes baked with anchovies, parsley, oregano and garlic has a remarkably modern feel.

Many new recipes of the time originated in religious orders, and Corrado's book probably circulated in these groups like a hot new best-seller. Pretty soon, the Jesuits of the Casa Professa in Rome were eating tomato frittata on meatless Fridays, the Celestine nuns of Trani were sipping *brodetto al pomodoro* and those in Catania were nibbling on *mortaretto*, a pastry stuffed with tomatoes and herbs. The horticulturalists of the day, particularly in Sardinia, also developed a technique to sun-dry tomatoes, which allowed their use

An 1870s engraving showing tomatoes, among other crops, being cultivated by peasants near Naples.

Sun-dried tomatoes in southern Italy.

during the winter months. Another Sardinian technique in which tomatoes were preserved as a vinegary condiment also became popular.[15]

By the nineteenth century, tomatoes had become so plentiful and cheap they could be hurled at public performers. One British gardener, John Claudius Loudon, noted that 'near Rome and Naples, whole fields are covered with it, and scarcely a dinner is served up in which it does not in some way or other form a part.'[16] In Naples this abundance was paradoxically matched by a decrease in meat and cereal consumption. In fact, the diet of the poor was largely vegetarian even if the vegetables were overripe or rotten.

After the Expedition of the Thousand, led in Sicily in 1860–61 by Giuseppe Garibaldi to conquer the region from

Bourbon rule, the tomato triumphantly spread throughout the whole peninsula, helping to unify and blend a motley collection of peoples. As Piero Camporesi wrote,

> The tomato had long been neglected in culinary practice, viewed almost with suspicion and relegated to a negligible role. Now, much more than the potato, it became a revolutionary new element that broke the mould of eighteenth-century Italian cooking.[17]

In other words, it became an edible symbol of reunification, and the start of the road towards large-scale cultivation.

Preservation

The simplest method used to preserve tomatoes, first documented in Sicily in 1868, was to sun-dry the entire plant, which was harvested before it had ripened completely. In this way, the tomatoes kept their sugar content through the following months. In time it also became common practice to chop up the fresh tomatoes, boil them for a long time, and filter out the seeds and skin: this dense, dark sauce, dried and regularly turned over in the sun, produced a red-black conserve that was shaped into loaves and wrapped in oiled paper.

Following a crisis in the 1880s when grain prices plunged, many farmers in the areas of Naples and Salerno in the south and around Parma and Piacenza in the north turned to tomatoes as a major crop. Thanks to the discoveries of Nicolas Appert, new technology enabled the Naples region to produce canned whole tomatoes; around Parma, ever more sophisticated factories focused on canning concentrate, paste, pulp and *passata*. The first company to process tomatoes there

Concentrated Italian tomato purée (paste).

was formed by a group of local farmers in 1874, and was called the Anonymous Society of Farmers for the Preparation of Tomato Conserve: as early as the 1880s, they were selling to the UK and Argentina.[18]

The market grew in the 1920s for *pelati*, whole, skinned tomatoes canned in their juice. Within a few years the San Marzano became the variety of choice, and approximately 140 firms were operating by 1925. Almost two-thirds of the output

was exported: the domestic market was limited because m
Italians found the price of dried pasta and tinned tomat
to be prohibitive. Eventually, however, brands such as C
were able to produce goods more cheaply and build ho
sales, as well as supply overseas markets with tinned tomat
paste and concentrate.

In the Mussolini years the 'cooking of conquest' wa
form of social engineering that promoted a certain cultu
and political outlook. Il Duce advocated less dependency
imports, stressing the importance of self-sufficiency wit
nutritional requirements and greater consumer discipline.
1936 a cookery contest attracted over 3,000 contestants,
proposing innovative ways to use canned tomatoes. One
the more outré recipes used tomato paste to glue toget
veal and bacon 'birds' on fried vegetable and potato 'nests

In the wake of the Second World War, southern Italia
seeking work in the north brought with them a craving for
familiar foods of their native regions. This inter-regio
exchange had always existed for the higher classes, l
now there was a wider commercial demand for foods t
otherwise would never have travelled, such as buffalo-m
mozzarella, olive oil – and sun-dried tomatoes.

Pasta, Pizza and Tomato Sauce

The union of pasta and tomato sauce now seems predestin
but it was neither immediate nor inevitable. Red took sor
time to appear in the palette of colours used by cooks throug
out Italy although, as Massimo Montanari wryly notes, it v
to become too much of a good thing.[20]

Francesco Leonardi in *Apicio moderno* (The Modern A
cius, 1790) had noted the difference between tomato pu

and tomato sauce,[21] but it was Pellegrino Artusi, in the great pan-Italian cookery book *La scienza in cucina e l'arte di mangiare bene* (Science in the Kitchen and the Art of Eating Well, 1891), who was probably the first popular writer to make a systematic distinction and define the composition of the latter. Piero Camporesi described Artusi as a 'precursor – indeed a pioneer – of the present, universal uniform (at times monotonous) homogenized diet which has plastered the whole peninsula with spaghetti and tomato sauce.' Camporesi also slyly comments that Artusi would probably have disowned his own book if he could have foreseen the end result.[22]

The pairing, at first, was slow to develop, and when it did the sauce was not centre stage in terms of written accounts. Perhaps it was assumed by nineteenth-century writers that

Pasta and tomato sauce.

Pizza Margherita.

no instruction was necessary. In 1837, for example, when Duke Ippolito Cavalcanti of Buonvicino published *Cucina teorico-practica* (The Theory and Practice of Cooking), he wrote that the secret of a successful dish of baked vermicelli with tomatoes was first to make a dense tomato sauce, but gave no directions how to do so because 'everyone knows how to make it', whether from fresh, preserved or sun-dried tomatoes.[23]

Neither is the year when bread met tomato to make a pizza prototype precisely known, although the Association Verace Pizza Napoletana dates the pizza marinara to 1734. Over the next century, tomatoes became so important to pizza-making around Naples that breeders developed special varieties such as the 'King Humbert', a trailing and now relatively rare variety that does not require staking.

In 1889 the new Italian queen Margherita was honoured in Naples with a red, green and white pizza, the colours of the national flag. Overnight it was an invented tradition; the 'pizza of unification', as Arthur Allen describes it.[24] Apart from the Roman *pizza bianca*, it is now rare to find a commercial pizza minus the ubiquitious, worldwide 'red sauce'.

Tomates provençales, or French stuffed tomatoes.

4
Elsewhere in Europe

When it came to learning to love the tomato, the French were slow off the starting block. The *Dictionnaire de Trévoux* (1704) reported that Italians ate tomatoes 'with salt, pepper, and oil, much as cucumbers', but they were still largely regarded as ornamental annuals. Although the Vilmorin-Andrieux seed catalogue of 1778 lists the tomato as a vegetable for the first time, in 1789 Rozier in *Cours d'agriculture* (Course in Agriculture) noted, 'This plant is mostly unknown by gardeners in the northern part of France and even if they are grown it is mostly from curiosity than practicality; but in Italy, Spain, in Provence and Languedoc, this fruit is much sought after.'[1]

That year was the start of the French Revolution, which also introduced the tomato to Paris. As the story goes, the comrades from Marseille were said to miss their beloved tomatoes so much that some enterprising restaurateurs saw an opportunity to bring Provençal cuisine to the capital. Initially they were very expensive, delicately displayed on wicker trays, but within a few years they were common and cheap enough to be piled high in large baskets in Les Halles. A recipe for tomato conserve from Carpentras in the Vaucluse dated 1795, which was unearthed by Barbara Santich, seems to be the first written French recipe for tomatoes so far discovered.[2]

Antique illustration of large early red tomato.

Grimod de La Reynière in the *Almanach des gourmands* (1803) remarked on the increasing availability of the 'pretty little fruit' and said that 'Excellent in sauces to accompany meats, chopped up in soups with rice, they can even be eaten as side dishes.' To underline the point he provided a recipe for stuffed tomatoes, possibly the first in print for this staple dish.[3]

In 1828 the French botanist and physician Michel Étienne Descourtilz was equally receptive to the tomato's virtues when he wrote,

> The resources which it offers the culinary art in the preparation of *ragouts* and *coulis*, have given it admittance to all the vegetable gardens in the vicinity of Paris. Its paste is conserved for the winter, by means of drying; then, when the vegetable resources are limited, in the middle of the winter, the tomato sauce appears on our

tables in a thousand ways – to serve in beef or mutton soups, to be associated with codfish and many other varieties of fish. One eats it in the colonies with *piment* and other aromatics to prevent inertia in the stomach. One preserves tomatoes in vinegar while they are young. Its culture demands a rich soil and humidity.[4]

The same year, a report in *The Gardener's Magazine* in London described a visit to the 'forcing department' of the Versailles kitchen garden: 'a stock of young tomato plants were ready to transplant into their pots to fruit during the winter, the fresh fruit being wanted throughout the year for soups, stews and sauces . . . tomatoes were supplied every day in the year'.[5]

When Alexandre Dumas' *Grand Dictionnaire de cuisine* was published after his death in 1870, the entry on the tomato

Late 19th-century label for bottled French tomatoes.

described it as 'a fruit which comes to us from the people of the south, who treat it with honour. Its flesh is eaten in purée form and its sweet juice is used in seasoning.'

Across the Channel, John Gerard was one of the first to grow tomatoes in England. In 1597 he reported the receipt of seeds from Spain and Italy but despite the fact that he knew tomatoes were eaten in southern Europe without people dropping dead, he followed the lead of the Flemish herbalist Dodoens (whose writings he casually plagiarized), who had commented a few years earlier, 'Some eat the fruits prepared and cooked with pepper, salt and oil. However, they provide little bodily sustenance, and this is itself noxious and pernicious.' Gerard took an equally negative view by describing them in his *Herball* as emitting a 'ranke and stinking savour' and possessing 'perhaps the highest degree of coldnesse'. And, in addition, any nourishment they yielded would be 'naught and corrupt'. Nonetheless, Gerard noted how they were prepared, boiled with pepper, salt and oil in Spain or mixed with oil, vinegar and pepper as a sauce for meat 'even as we in these cold countries do Mustard'. He also chanced upon another variety that produced yellow fruit, but still remained unimpressed.[6]

John Parkinson in *Paradisi in sole paradisus terrestris* (A Garden of Pleasant Flowers, 1629) kept up the theme: '[they are] of a faire pale reddish colour, or somewhat deeper, like unto an Orenge, full of slimie juice and waterie pulp.'[7] Over a century later, John Hill noted in his gardening manual *Eden* that 'Few eat this, but it is agreeable in soups. Those who are us'd to eat with the Portuguese Jews know the value of it.'[8]

Tomatoes were, indeed, to remain a decorative novelty or medicinal ingredient for over two centuries, deemed to have no place in the kitchen: they upset the stomach, caused faintness and apoplexy, brought on colic and diarrhoea and

HOW BIDDY SERVED THE TOMATOES UNDRESSED.
"Indade, Ma'am, an I'll not take off another stitch, if I lose me place."

Cartoon of Biddy serving the tomatoes undressed, from an American advertisement for Lemon Chill Tonic, *c.* 1850–1900.

English recipes, including stuffed tomatoes and salads with tomatoes, from *Smiley's Cook Book and Universal Household Guide* (1895).

worse. Although Philip Miller of the Chelsea Physic Garden did admit in 1754 that they were much used to give 'an agreeable Acid to the Soup', and a 1758 supplement to *The Art of Cookery* by Hannah Glasse included a recipe 'To Dress Haddock after the Spanish Way' that featured 'love apples', and though Jane Austen enthusiastically endorsed them,[9] tomatoes were little favoured at most British tables until the end of the century.

The transformation to an everyday item, however, was then rapid and only twenty years later 'Tomato sauce was put on anything sent to the table.' The seal of approval came when tomatoes were included as ingredients of daily usage in the *Encyclopaedia Britannica*, 'either boiled in soups or broths, or served up boiled as garnishes to flesh-meats.'[10]

By 1820 *The Times* confessed, 'Love-apples are now to be seen in great abundance at all our vegetable markets.' Although the writer admitted that the middle and lower classes had not yet adopted them, he argued that 'within this last few years it has come into great use with all our best cooks.'[11] The first two printed English recipes for tomato sauce came from Maria Rundell (1806) and, a decade later, William Kitchiner, who also made a 'tomata or love-apple sauce', stewing them with gravy before pressing through a tamis and boiling them thick with lemon juice.

Christopher Stocks suggests that the British market for tomatoes was slow to take off for the simple reason that 'being relatively tender, tomatoes are not naturally suited to the British climate'.[12] Certainly commercial cultivation was not really possible until the late nineteenth century, when the glass needed for large greenhouses became cheap enough for them to be constructed in market gardens in the southeast of England. At the end of the century, Worthing was the tomato capital of Britain, closely challenged by the Channel Islands.

Tinned soups were particularly popular as provisions during long sea journeys, although they were very expensive. Andrew F. Smith quotes the fascinating fact that the contents of some tins left over from early expeditions were analysed 114 years later and were discovered to be neither rancid nor lacking in vitamin D.[13] By the turn of the century pre-processed tomato products had become everyday items. An Army & Navy Stores catalogue of 1907 lists tomato chutneys, tinned tomatoes, tomato ketchup, bottled tomatoes, tomato conserve, tomato purée and tomato soups.[14]

The British had fallen in love with the love apple.

Suspicion

Almost as soon as tomatoes arrived in Europe they were regarded with suspicion. It was claimed that tomatoes made your teeth fall out. The smell was said to drive people insane. Many thought them just too ugly to eat. Plus there was the fear of poisoning by strange fruit.

The Paduan physician Giovanni Domenico Sala, writing in 1628, described tomatoes and aubergines as 'strange and horrible things' that 'a few unwise people' were willing to eat (so someone was eating them!). But we should not be too quick to ridicule the reluctant. As David Gentilcore suggests, there were reasons for this: in much of Europe there was little knowledge of how to correctly cultivate them; their trailing habit was inauspicious; the plants did indeed have stems and leaves that may be toxic when eaten raw; they had little flavour or aroma and were highly acidic; and they were not very filling, so of little benefit in a subsistence diet.[15]

And there were religious concerns. 'There is nothing more evil', wrote Abbot Chiari during the tomato naissance of the mid-1700s, 'than [the growing habit] of foods that are covered in drugs [spices] from America.' Sauces encouraged men not just to eat but to eat like gluttons. Stewart Lee Allen described the satanic dangers vividly: 'The tomato's unearthly brilliance, its zesty flavour, its lugubriously dripping succulence, were all anathema to the clergy. It "inflamed passions" in ways that the grubby brown potato could hardly be accused of doing.'[16]

In northern Europe, however, there may have been more plausible reasons for the slow acceptance of the tomato. The Little Ice Age, which lasted in Europe for about four hundred years until the nineteenth century, had particularly cold and snowy winters and short, unreliable growing seasons, so cultivating tomatoes, especially out of doors, must have been a considerable challenge.

In addition, apart from the fact that they were delicate and difficult to transport, old varieties of tomato, adapted as they were to warm climates, may well have tasted disagreeable if planted outside their comfort zone.[17] It did not help either that these horticultural novelties were defined according to the received wisdom of 'humours' as cold and wet foods that were harmful to human health.[18] They were said to cause gout and were also held to be lacking in both nourishment and substance.[19]

Among some sections of society, old beliefs died hard. In *Lark Rise to Candleford*, Flora Thompson recorded the plant's first arrival in the English hamlet when 'tommytoes' were widely regarded as 'nasty, horrid things . . . as only gentry can eat'. Even today, the fear of tomatoes, or lycopersicoaphobia, can leave its victims feeling queasy. I suggest they avoid the cult 1978 film *Attack of the Killer Tomatoes*.

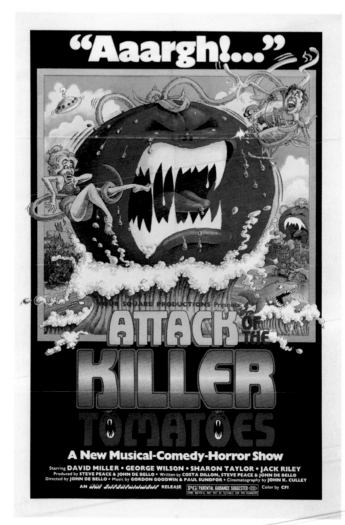

Poster for the film *Attack of the Killer Tomatoes* (1978).

A Jewish Perspective

In Eastern Europe some communities of Hassidic Jews once refused to believe tomatoes could be kosher and were convinced that because of their vivid colour they must contain forbidden blood.[20] There are many tales of domestic discord and culture shock that ensued when Jews from tomato-avoiding regions wed tomato-eating spouses.[21] Even then, as Joan Nathan wryly notes, 'Jews either avoided eating tomatoes or cooked them to death as they did meat.'[22]

One early immigrant to Palestine in 1925 remembered his astonishment at seeing Jewish people eating tomatoes: 'The tomato, which in Poland we saw growing in the window boxes of the Christians, and which we therefore dubbed the "Christians' apple" or the *treife* apple was eaten here by the Jews as well.' Isaac Kumer, the Galician hero of the novelist S. Y. Agnon's *Only Yesterday*, who arrived at the turn of the twentieth century, also had a hard time recognizing the tomato as proper food. To him, the tomato was a 'fool's apple', as it was called back home.[23] Allen Ginsberg in his poem *Kaddish, Part 1*, dedicated to his mother, recalls her arrival from Russia as a little girl 'eating the first poisonous tomatoes of America'.

The tomato became the symbol of both the individual's commitment to the Zionist enterprise and the agricultural collective. In the words of the 1926 hit song 'Tomato':

> Ho, ho, ho, our land is poor
> Let every living creature sing
> the tomato anthem.
> Tomato, tomato!
> Just yesterday we came off the boat
> and already you feature in our borscht,
> our salad, and our meatballs . . .

Israeli tomato and cucumber salad.

> It's tomatoes, only tomatoes
> from the moshav of Bnei Brak to [Kibbutz] Degania . . .[24]

Interestingly, in Jewish law, before eating tomatoes one should recite the blessing over the 'fruit of the tree' not the 'fruit of the earth'. It was a distinction that loomed large in the history of the tomato, especially in nineteenth-century America.

5
Back to America

In *A Tramp Abroad* (1880), Mark Twain describes both his detestation of European cuisine and the American dishes he most missed, from oyster soup to peach cobbler. In a long list of foods he dreams of eating as soon as he steps off the steamer are sliced tomatoes with sugar or vinegar, and stewed tomatoes. His love of the tomato was honed on a childhood turkey hunt when he came across an abandoned log cabin with a garden full of perfectly ripe tomatoes. 'I ate them ravenously,' he wrote, 'though I had never liked them before. Not more than two or three times since have I tasted anything that was so delicious as those tomatoes.' However, in true Twain discombobulating style he adds, 'I surfeited myself with them, and did not taste another one until I was in middle life. I can eat them now, but I do not like the look of them.'[1]

He was not alone. Tomatoes, on their return trip to America, were viewed by many with as much suspicion as they were on their arrival in Europe. Geographic isolation, culinary conservatism and seasonal limitations slowed their spread. Most colonists were not interested in adapting to new foods but in finding new land to plant the old and familiar ones. As historian Alfred Crosby explained, 'the whole migration of

Spaniards, Portuguese, and the others who followed them across the Atlantic . . . depended upon their ability to "Europeanize" the flora and fauna of the New World.'[2]

As a result, in both Jamestown and Plymouth, two of the earliest English settlements, colonists faced starvation conditions for several years until they learned to adapt their diets to the culinary options available in the New World. In the ironic words of food scholar Waverley Root, 'The first settlers had come upon a land of plenty. They nearly starved in it.'[3] Even then, many 'turned their backs on most of the new foods, often refusing to eat them until after Europe had accepted them and reimported them to the land of their origin'.[4]

There was indeed a genuine fear of eating vegetables, as these were commonly rinsed and washed in polluted water or

Sliced green tomatoes in an egg wash.

consumed in summer when illness could spread rapidly. But this explanation has been blown out of proportion and it is more likely that they were seen simply as curiosities or decorative additions to the garden. Others described them as 'odious and repulsive smelling berries'.[5]

The apocryphal story of Robert Gibbon Johnson, the first man in America to publicly eat a supposedly poisonous tomato, on the Salem courthouse steps in 1820, is just that – apocryphal. Although one hesitates to spoil a good story with the facts, there is no primary evidence to validate it. Andrew F. Smith explains that the legend stuck because it rings true and is impossible to disprove. It may well be that the residents of Salem saw the tale as a good opportunity to get on a bandwagon and promote their home town.[6]

Smith not only definitively debunks this self-perpetuating story but the hundreds of similar 'introduction by great-man' accounts. He casts a sceptical eye also over the veracity and authenticity of the claims of various cultural groups, from Spanish settlers and missionaries to French Huguenot refugees, English colonists and African slaves.[7] Even Thomas Jefferson, who had been growing, and presumably eating, 'tomatas' since 1781, got in on the act by crediting a London immigrant named Dr Sequeyra of Jewish-Portuguese heritage with their introduction in the mid-eighteenth century. The truth is probably a piecemeal combination of them all.

There were certainly early issues of high perishability and preservation but, as these technical problems were overcome, there was no stopping the tomato's advance into culinary society. There are indications tomatoes were grown in the Carolinas at the end of the seventeenth century, and by the middle of the eighteenth they were found throughout the country, especially in Florida, New Mexico, Texas and California – and not just for ornamental use.

James Peale, *Balsam Apple and Vegetables*, c. 1820, oil on canvas. One of only a handful of still-lifes painted in the U.S. before the mid-19th century known to show tomatoes. James Peale was the uncle of the painter Raphaelle Peale.

Around 1795, a large red tomato appears in an American painting for the first time: *Still-life with Vegetables and Fruit* was painted by Raphaelle Peale and depicts a tomato, raised from French seeds, with a segmented, heavily lobed and rather flattened shape.[8] Bernard M'Mahon's *American Gardener's Calendar* (1806) stated that the tomato was 'much cultivated for its fruit, in soups and sauces, to which it imparts an agreeable acid flavour'. As time went on, references and recipes increased in cookery manuscripts (it is worth remembering that these often lagged decades behind actual kitchen practices).

British influence on the American colonial kitchen through immigration and cookbooks encouraged the cultivation of 'love apples', stimulated by the concurrent work of seedsmen, gardeners, farmers and botanists. French and Creole refugees, especially from today's Haiti, also helped spread the word, as did the wave of French restaurants that opened in America in the mid-1800s.[9]

Robert Buist reflected in the 1847 gardening manual *The Family Kitchen Gardener*,

> In taking a retrospect of the past eighteen years, there is no vegetable on the catalogue that has obtained such popularity in so short a period . . . In 1828–9 it was almost detested . . . It now occupies as great a surface of ground as Cabbage, and is cultivated the length and breadth of the country.[10]

His words were echoed by the editor of the *Florida Agriculturist*, who recalled, a few decades after first tasting a tomato, that anyone 'who would have predicted that the tomato would ever become popular as an esculent or to be used in any utilitarian way except as a gratification to the eye, would have been

Tomato ices were popular in the 19th century and have seen a comeback in recent years.

A U.S. government Victory Gardens poster, 1940s.

set down at once as daft or visionary'.[11] Nonetheless, in 1899 a well-known food writer, Christine Terhune Herrick, used her syndicated newspaper column to lament that 'few persons appreciate the full value of the tomato in the family bill of fare.' Americans, she noted, used the tomato to make salads or soups, or perhaps might serve them scalloped or stewed. In doing so, 'they have hardly touched upon its possibilities.'[12]

Congress soon took notice of the fledgling industry: taxation, in other words. In 1883 the Tariff Act was introduced to impose a 10 per cent duty on imported vegetables. The crucial issue in the subsequent test case, which involved the import of tomatoes from the West Indies, was whether the tomato was to be defined as a vegetable or a fruit. For years the case was argued in the Supreme Court before judgement came down on the side of common usage over botanical correctness – for the sake of tax purposes. The answer was a boon to quizmasters forever after, in that technically the tomato may be a fruit but in everyday parlance it is sold and bought on the vegetable side of the counter.

As tomatoes became ever more fashionable, they were praised for their delicious taste, versatility and nutritional virtues. They were considered the queen of American farmers' markets, and were to become arguably America's most popular 'vegetable'. During the short time the u.s. was in the First World War, many Americans grew 'victory gardens', most of which included tomatoes.

Italians in America

In the film *Nuovomondo* (2006), director Emanuele Crialese showed America as imagined by Sicilian peasants preparing to emigrate in the hope of escaping their misery and hunger. For them, America is the land of plenty, where one swims in lakes of milk, coins fall from the sky and gigantic tomatoes and carrots are grown. The reality, of course, was somewhat different.

Although the tomato was already widely consumed in nineteenth-century Italy, it was only in the 1850s that it began to be served as a sauce on pasta. Those immigrants arriving before 1900 were really the first generation to be familiar with a dish of spaghetti and tomato sauce. Yet no other group were as important as the Italians to tomato culture in the United States up to the Second World War. Ironically, the first immigrants brought with them distinct regional cuisines, reflecting the fact that at the time Italy was more a political construction than a cultural reality. As they shared their culinary traditions and found themselves with more money to spend on food, a New World Italian cuisine emerged. Growers, producers, distributors, stores and restaurants all helped produce an image of a unified, national Italian cuisine. In the words of historian Hasia R. Diner, they 'wound the fabric of the community around food'.[13]

Eventually local entrepreneurs developed their own versions of foodstuffs. By the late 1930s, a dozen Italian American companies producing tomato products in California exceeded the total volume of tomato products imported from Italy. The circle was completed as Italian Americans exported these foodstuffs back to Italy. Eventually the staples of the Italian diet – pizza and pasta – became global in their appeal as simple and satisfying meals.

This was the background to the ubiquitous spaghetti in a can sold under the brand name of Chef Boy-Ar-Dee that originated with Ettore Boiardi, a chef from Piacenza. He had an Italian restaurant in Cleveland and decided to can and distribute his sauce, packaging it with dried spaghetti and grated

Mama Melrose's Ristorante Italiano at Disney Hollywood Studios.

cheese. He became hugely successful, even supplying the u.s. Army during the Second World War.

Arguably, if ironically, the most important innovation of Italians in America was to combine spaghetti with hamburger meatballs in a 'red gravy' tomato sauce. This became the quintessential Italian dish that was the signature item of most

Italian restaurants by the 1920s. It was not intended solely to attract an American audience. Writing in his 1950s memoir, *Love and Dishes*, restaurateur Niccolo de Quattrociocchi recalled, upon first trying the dish, finding it 'extremely satisfying' and feeling that 'someone in Italy should invent [it] for the Italians over there'.[14]

The Healthy Tomato

Ever since Francisco Hernández noted in 1570 that the tomato was used in Mexico for medicinal purposes, it has been seen as a potential source of New World remedies for Old World ailments and used to treat every manner of ailment from headaches, earaches, stomach aches and mumps to 'the itch'. Its efficacy, however, has not always been proven.

Like sugar and cola, the adoption of the tomato in the popular diet was preceded by medicinal claims. Pronouncements by the controversial nineteenth-century American Dr John C. Bennett were wildly exaggerated, preposterous even, hailing tomatoes as successful in the treatment of diarrhoea and dyspepsia. They were also good, he avowed, for citizens travelling west or south, as they would save them 'from the danger attendant upon those violent bilious attacks to which almost all unacclimated persons are liable'.[15]

Opinion polarized, with some doctors insisting they cured just about every illness in the medical dictionary, others debunking it all as total quackery. As the century went on, however, more people subscribed to the view they were a kind of cure-all wonder drug.[16] One enthusiastic American newspaper correspondent wrote in 1837, 'time would fail me to enumerate all the diseases in which its virtues as a remedial agent have been tested.'[17]

Tomato soup was particularly praised as a healthy dish. Horatio Woods, a leading Philadelphia physician, noted it was a 'very elegant and cheap soup, suitable to many cases of invalids', and it was endorsed by Ella Kellogg, wife of the co-inventor of the breakfast cereal cornflakes.[18]

Andrew F. Smith describes this as the first wave of tomato mania: the second came in the 1830s and '40s, when such claims were concretely expressed in the form of tomato medicines and pills, an enthusiasm propelled by an increasing awareness of the importance of vitamins and minerals in a healthy diet. He notes that over 6,000 advertisements for tomato pills have been located, and these are probably only a fraction of the total number published: nor did this figure include the hundreds of articles and recipes that extolled the panacea of the healthy tomato, as well as reports of miracle cures from liver disease to cholera. In time this acclaim subsided and while miracles were struck off the list and doubt lingered on, the tomato was recognized as a wholesome food with nutritional benefits, although suggesting that their consumption would improve public morals, as one publication pronounced, was perhaps taking things a bit far.

Tomatoes undoubtedly have various health-promoting properties and carry a significant amount of vitamin C and carotenoids that, according to the American Institute for Cancer Research, may prevent the development of some cancers. In particular, they contain lycopene, a carotene that gives tomatoes and other red or pink fruit their red colour and is an antioxidant that attacks free radicals suspected of triggering malignant cell growth.[19]

A 2016 Spanish study noted that tomato sauce enriched with olive oil has greater beneficial effects for cardiovascular health than either raw tomato or tomato sauce taken alone.[20] The following year Italian scientists working for the Sbarro

Health Research Organization found that whole tomato extracts from two different southern Italian cultivars inhibited gastric cancer cell growth, paving the way for future studies aimed at implementing lifestyle habits not only for prevention but potentially as a support to conventional therapies. Interestingly the authors say their effects seem unrelated to specific components such as lycopene, but rather suggest tomatoes should be considered in their entirety.[21]

Oral consumption of lycopene, in a German study, has also been shown to protect the skin against the harmful

Advertisement for Libby's tomato juice, emphasizing the health attributes of the food, 1947.

effects of uv radiation and stave off wrinkles (though is no substitute for sunscreen).[22] Ironically, in view of the history of tomato pills and medications, lycopene capsules also have a niche market in the prevention of heart disease – although it's perfectly possible and probably preferable to obtain the nutrient from diet alone. Scientists at the University of Iowa have discovered that a natural compound found in green tomatoes (and apples) helps combat a protein that causes muscle weakness and loss during ageing.[23]

And as well as cancer, tomatoes have also been linked (if not always conclusively) to reducing the risk of high blood pressure and diabetes, even in the form of tinned tomatoes, ketchup and tomato-paste-topped pizza. Ketchup, however, is not a vegetable: the concept of it as belonging to a basic food group was a cost-cutting measure proposed by the Reagan administration that was never destined to fly. While a spoonful of ketchup might help the hot dog go down, it has little to add to a healthy diet. Although not without some nutritional value, helped by commercial sugar level reductions, it comes nowhere near the benefits of eating a fresh tomato.[24]

Tomatoes are a natural functional food, but today they can also contain high levels of pesticide residue. Their potassium content means they should be consumed in moderation by people taking beta-blockers or with kidney problems. Needless to say, the benefits of tomato juice are lowered if it contains added salt, sugar or chemicals.

The jury's out on the Bloody Mary.

Boys working in a cannery, unloading freight cars full of new tomato cans, Indianapolis, 1908.

6
Soup and Ketchup

Ever since it was noticed that the summer produced a glut of tomatoes, the need to conserve a perishable product for off-season consumption became a problem to be solved with an equal excess of drying, bottling, pickling and paste-making solutions.[1]

Bottling and canning were two of the main ways to preserve tomatoes. In France, Nicolas Appert developed a technique in the early nineteenth century of stewing, straining and sealing tomatoes in bottles that were then boiled in a water bath and hermetically sealed. Soon, commercial bottling was taking place in the United States, and before long Harrison W. Crosby from New Jersey innovated packing hand-soldered tin pails with tomatoes. A skilled tinsmith could turn out fifty or sixty cans a day, and to promote his product, he even sent samples to Queen Victoria and President James K. Polk.

By 1850, new machinery enabled two unskilled men to produce 1,500 tins a day. The U.S. Civil War increased the demand for canned goods to feed soldiers: when the latter returned home, they brought with them a taste for the peas, corn and tomatoes they had grown used to. Technology became increasingly sophisticated and farmers who had planted acres of tomatoes in New Jersey to meet the demand

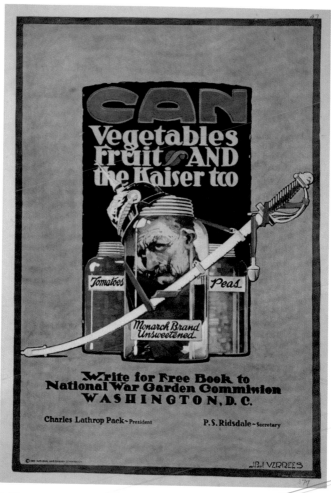

A First World War poster encouraging Americans to preserve foods, featuring Kaiser Wilhelm of Germany in a glass jar.

Home canning was encouraged in the U.S. throughout the Second World War.

HOME CANNING

Tomatoes

SELECTION
AND
PREPARATION

• Choose fresh, firm, ripe tomatoes.
• Watch out for decay ....one bad spot may spoil a whole batch.

• Wash thoroughly

• Dip in scalding hot water then in cold .... for easy peeling.

for early crops were now able to divert the subsequent glut into canned goods: the tomato emerged as a market leader. As demand increased, prices dropped.[2]

By 1876, however, the situation had gone into reverse and supply far outstripped demand. Economic depression and crop failure played a part and many canneries in New Jersey closed. Maryland took up the slack and started a rivalry between the two states that was to continue for some time. At the turn of the century, more tomatoes were canned than any other fruit or vegetable, and by the 1920s the process was fully automated.

Arguably, minimally processed canned tomatoes were a stimulus for culinary creativity and curiousity, unlike convenience foods such as crackers and ready-baked bread. After John L. Mason introduced domestic glass canning jars in 1858, the process of putting up fruit and vegetables became much easier; the self-sealing jars were not only safer and more reliable but were also reusable.[3]

Tomato Soup

As Andrew F. Smith notes, the earliest culinary use of tomatoes in Britain and America was to provide an extra note of acidity, juicy texture and colour to other ingredients. In Mary Randolph's *Virginia Housewife* (1824), for example, tomatoes featured in recipes for veal, barley and okra soups.

Gradually, the proportion of tomato content increased, and Smith pinpoints the first real American tomato or 'tomata' soup recipe to a cookbook appearance in 1832.[4] From then on, tomato soup started to climb the social scale, appearing on all manner of festive and celebratory menus. Regular and 'fancy' tomato soups diversified further into cream of tomato or tomato bisque, tomato bouillon, tomato consommé and the combination of tomato soup with other key ingredients.

Although many consumers used canned tomatoes to make soup, the benefits of ready-made soup soon became apparent. James H. W. Huckins of Boston was the first soup canner in 1876 but others were quick to follow his lead, such as the Franco-American Food Company, renowned for their 'French' soups, which was later sold to the Campbell Soup Company.

In the late nineteenth century the Anderson Preserving Company in New Jersey specialized in processing tomatoes, especially their 'Celebrated Beefsteak Tomato', which, according to their slogan, was 'so large that only one was packed to a can'. After ownership passed to Joseph Campbell, the latter began to produce a wide range of goods, including a ready-to-serve soup.

Condensed soups were the next big step forward. They had clear advantages: lower manufacturing costs, less storage space for the smaller cans and reduced transport bills. All you had to do was add water, heat and serve. The concept was not altogether new but a Campbell family member, a chemist named John T. Dorrance, took it into mass production. The first five flavours, including tomato, were released in 1897. They were sold as embodying savings in time and labour, economy, nutrition, ease of preparation and versatility. As the brilliant strap-line from an unsung advertising genius put it, 'One Taste is worth a Thousand Words!'

The impact was enormous. As the authors of *Exploring the Tomato* expressed it so succinctly, 'Tomato ketchup and soup were pioneering the mass production of food. It was Fordism before Ford. Tomatoes before cars.'[5] Tinned tomato soup was to become a legend in a can, a commodity based on mass production, standardization, content regulation, pricing structures, distribution networks and innovative new ways of marketing and advertising, with campaign concepts such as the iconic Campbell Soup Kids, sponsorship of popular radio and TV programmes, and cookery books and pamphlets. Campbell's Condensed Tomato Soup soon was found in a huge range of recipes, including the wildly popular Tomato Soup Cake. A recipe for the equally famous Aspic Salad was originally printed in the *Ladies' Home Journal* and later featured in *The Alice B. Toklas Cook Book* (1954).

For decades, housewives had been planning and shopping for pre-decided menus. Increasingly, the home-maker needed to do neither. 'Emergency' substitutes filled the nation's cupboards. The *reductio ad absurdum* of this, as Harvey Levenstein cleverly points out, was a recipe for 'Emergency Cream of Tomato Soup', for use when the cans had run out: one cup of diluted thin cream or condensed milk to which three tablespoons of catsup were added.[6]

The famous red-and-white colour of the tin, with its uncluttered style and clean lines, had replaced the somewhat sombre black-and-orange label in 1898. It was an important design innovation that subliminally promoted the virtues of time and space-saving convenience, enhanced by the gold medal the company won at the 1900 Paris Exposition Universelle and still displayed on the label today. Decades later, it inspired Andy Warhol to reinvent the traditional still-life of natural objects such as fruit and flowers in the form of

The Royal Scottish Academy decorated with images of Andy Warhol's famous Campbell's soup cans, 2008.

Harvesting tomatoes by hand is laborious but protects the tomato; mechanical harvesting is best suited to canning and processing.

manufactured objects commonly placed in a 'pile 'em high and sell 'em cheap' setting.

An early diversification into tomato juice was an instant hit with the American public and the company developed a suitable tomato for the job, launching a successful marketing drive in 1931. The end of Prohibition was celebrated with the new Bloody Mary cocktail. As the firm grew it could enjoy economies of scale and invest in state-of-the-art equipment: in 1935 the Campbell's Soup factory in Camden, New Jersey, could produce ten million cans of soup in one day.

Breeding a tomato suitable for canning and soup-making had, in fact, begun much earlier. The right balance of acid and sugar, a thick skin, a deep shape, a rich colour, ripening from the inside out and resistance to disease were all desirable qualities. It took many years but eventually the Rutgers tomato, developed in New Jersey, was pronounced 'of unexcelled quality'. It was to become one of the most widely grown tomatoes in the USA until it was superseded in the 1950s by varieties that could be mechanically harvested.

Tomato Ketchup

Years ago, when I had occasion to visit several households in the old textile towns of northeast Lancashire where the ranks of terraced stone houses are now largely occupied by families from rural regions of Pakistan, I was struck by a singular addition to the dining table. At least, so it seemed to my Eurocentric, middle-class mind: it was the tomato ketchup bottle that took pride of place among the home-made samosas, juicy kebabs and aromatic rice dishes. I was shocked until I came to realize that the Heinz Ketchup bottle was a badge of arrival in an alien country, an exotic emblem of, if not assimilation, then at least accommodation in a world that to many of the women, at least, was as disorientating as Disneyland.

It also provoked an ironic reflection on how the spicy sauce had finally come full circle. Ketchup recipes were first published in England during the early eighteenth century based on a long-lasting condiment traders and colonists had grown used to in East and Southeast Asia. *Kētsiap* or *kecap* was used in various guises throughout these regions but as soybeans, one of the original ingredients, were not found in Europe, cooks substituted anchovies, mushrooms, walnuts and oysters. In the process they fashioned a different flavour profile from the original strained liquid, which became tangy with vinegar and lightly sweetened.[7] However, there was still no clear distinction between ketchups, sauces, relishes, pickles and chutneys.

Tomatoes are thought to be an American contribution to the genre. The terms *catsup* or *catchup* increasingly appear in the late eighteenth and early nineteenth centuries, in a thicker and less vinegary version than their British counterparts. The first known mention of tomato ketchup was a recipe printed in James Mease's *Archives of Useful Knowledge* in 1812, published in Philadelphia. Andrew F. Smith also notes that during the early nineteenth century the terms 'tomato sauce' and 'tomato ketchup' were practically interchangeable, although the latter was meant as a long-lasting preserve and the former intended to be served shortly after preparation.

Mary Randolph in *The Virginia Housewife* (1824) offered seventeen recipes using tomatoes, including two for tomato marmalade and one for catsup, and the New England cookbook author Lydia Maria Child wrote in *The American Frugal Housewife* (1833), 'the best sort of catsup is made from tomatoes.' Elisabeth Rozin notes that as the tomato is a prolific crop, its excess made it an obvious choice for preservation. Further, the English regarded it more as a fruit than a vegetable, 'sweetening and spicing it in the same way they flavoured apples or berries', especially once cheap, refined sugar was unleashed into the Anglo-American world.[8]

Making ketchup, however, was a long, messy affair and once it became commercially available in the 1850s as a by-product of the canning industry, it is easy to see why home production declined practically to zero. It was less expensive, less time-consuming and more convenient to buy in a store than make it from scratch. By 1896 tomato ketchup had become America's favourite sauce. The *New York Tribune* crowned it as the national condiment of the United States, available on every table in the land. Smith notes that over eight hundred ketchups have been identified as having been manufactured before 1915, but this figure is probably only a fraction of the total number.

The criteria for a good American ketchup also changed along with public taste. Homemade was perceived as lumpy

Sicilian marzipan tomatoes.

and dull in colour; commercial was vivid and thick, with plenty of sugar, vinegar and salt, and used both in prepared dishes and as a condiment. Recipes for tomato ketchup also indicate the diversity in taste profiles that could be achieved by mixing tomatoes with a variety of ingredients such as onions, mace, cloves, nutmeg and black pepper, as well as brown sugar. Meat remained dominant on American plates, and tomato sauces and ketchups proved vital to salvaging dishes that were over-cooked, utilized poor cuts of meat or generally lacked flavour.

In the same way that pasta and tomato sauce became inextricably linked with Italian and Italian American cooking, so ketchup and hamburgers shared a similar destiny in the story of u.s. cuisine, along with their close relationship with hot dogs and fries. As one of Heinz Ketchup's legendary, witty advertising lines went, 'Take me to your burger!' Their union represented a democratic, down-to-earth, no-frills national character, open to all.

In Pennsylvania, in the second half of the nineteenth century, Henry J. Heinz had launched a pickle and horseradish-preserving company. After a bumpy beginning, the company flourished, expanding its product line, and in 1876 he introduced tomato ketchup. As Smith describes, 'By 1890 the company had hit upon the now world famous combination of the keystone label, the neck band, the screw cap and the octagonal-shaped ketchup bottle.'[9] Fifteen years later Heinz was producing over five million bottles per annum; a year later this had passed twelve million.

Advertising was the key to success. Heinz displayed its products at fairs across America and on streetcars and billboards, and even built an ocean pier in Atlantic City to offer cooking demonstrations, free samples and lectures. In 1900 the company erected New York's first large neon sign, a six-storey-high bottle of their tomato ketchup. In the 1920s and '30s, their adroit marketing was based on the themes of

Smooth, uniform, appetizing. **No preservatives.**

TOMATO SOUP. The secret of its goodness ot only in the high grade of tomatoes used, but in careful blending with pure, rich cream and spices ir own grinding. The most delicious of purees d there's none like Heinz. **No preservatives.**

All sold under positive guarantee of purity and action or grocer refunds money.

Heinz Kitchens—always open—annually ive 30,000 visitors. Those who cannot e will enjoy our instructive klet on Heinz methods Heinz foods. t free.

J. HEINZ COMPANY
w York   Pittsburgh
   Chicago   London

PURE FOOD
57
HEINZ
VARIETIES
PRODUCTS

Advert for a variety of Heinz products, including soup and ketchup, from the *Boston Cooking School* magazine, 1908.

A tomato-shaped ketchup dispenser.

professionalism, all-tomato composition and widespread popularity: 'The Favorite Ketchup of 110 nations!' Later, cooking with 'red magic' played an increasing role in pushing sales, and a 1950s 'Cook with Ketchup Contest' resulted in the first all-ketchup recipe book, which contained such gems as 'Liver Loaf Highland Pot Roast' and 'Crimson Fruit Cake'.

Finding the right tomato for the product was as important as it was with soup. At first, large-fruited varieties were used but these tended to be both watery and lacking in pulp. Some were favoured for their high yield, others because of their deep red hues, but the hunt was on for a tomato that was disease-resistant, did not crack when ripe, was firm and well-coloured and produced a 'thick and rich' ketchup. With the advent of mechanical harvesting, other desirable qualities included fruit that matured all at the same time. From as early as 1926, Heinz supplied plants to contract growers, and their employees supervised cultivation.

Today, Heinz is not only one of the world's largest food companies, but is the largest ketchup producer, producing more than one billion ounces per year in bottles, plastic squeezies and containers large and small. It flies the scarlet flag for the American experience, and is a genuine culinary expression of the national melting pot. Yet, *O tempora o mores!* In recent years Mexican salsa, composed of tomatoes, chilli peppers, onions and seasoning, has become even more popular than ketchup in the USA. The Aztecs would have smiled.

For decades, Garrison Keillor's radio programme *A Prairie Home Companion* featured advertisements from 'The Ketchup Advisory Board', a fictional industry group promoting tomato ketchup for its 'natural mellowing agents'. Behaviour became erratic and impulsive without regular helpings of ketchup; only then would mellowness return. It was, of course, a skit, but it struck a hugely popular chord.

An advertisement for an early tomato variety, from the Moore & Simon's *Seed Buyer's Guide* of 1902.

7
Glasshouses and Beyond

Hot beds and glasshouses were designed as a way to protect young plants from the cold until they could be transplanted: they also helped the market gardener maximize an early crop of tomatoes. The former were generally heated by copious amounts of fermenting horse manure, the latter typically by burning fuel, which allowed a longer cultivation period.

Hot beds were at first used to grow produce for private personal consumption or as aristocratic status symbols. The introduction in the early nineteenth century of sheet glass, which was more transparent and thus let in more light, was revolutionary. In 1837 Sir Joseph Paxton built a huge conservatory at Chatsworth, followed by the Crystal Palace in which the Great Exhibition was held: such innovations received a great boost when the glass taxes were repealed in 1845, and young men came in large numbers from Belgium and the Netherlands to learn about the new industry.[1]

From the estates of the upper classes, tomato-growing moved down the scale to amateur middle-class gardeners. In the 1920s and '30s in the UK, more working-class people gained access to allotments and the suburban practice of keeping a small greenhouse in the garden became increasingly widespread. It was becoming a permanent home for a

Greenhouse Builders

Don't Let This Past Winter

Early commercial greenhouses were a boon to growers as the sheet glass kept the plants warm but allowed light to reach them.

year-round forced tomato crop, not just a stagepost in the plants' growth.

In the commercial world, especially in America, the increasing demand for fresh tomatoes influenced farmers in their efforts to improve varieties and develop an ever-earlier harvest or a longer season. In a 1908 advertisement for May's 'First of All Tomatoes', the seed house proclaimed it 'The Earliest in the World', promising it would ripen 'a week to ten days ahead of any other known variety.'[2]

Although by no means the only variable, the early tomato became a distinct category and some negative aspects, including smaller size and less attractive appearance, were overlooked in the aim of getting tomatoes to the market and kitchen table as quickly as possible. Quality was often the price to pay. One writer argued in 1925 that a 'craze for early stuff' meant 'the urban New Yorker is willing to pay 15 to 30 cents a pound for the pale pink, anaemic, sweat house ripened tomatoes of the premature birth, simply because they come in January and can't see 50 cents value in a bushel of *real* tomatoes in July.'[3]

Outdoor-grown Southern tomatoes, however, were not always better, picked hard and green in order to get to distant northern markets without damage and sprayed with ethylene gas to induce ripening. The result was a tomato with a mealy, starchy texture not helped by refrigeration. Whatever the drawbacks and disadvantages, from now on consumers expected and were able to to enjoy the year-round tomato.[4]

The downside, of course, was frequent loss of flavour. Commercial growers still shudder to remember the Great German Water Bomb Scandal of the 1980s, which nearly destroyed the Dutch industry. German consumers, who were the largest market, wanted the lowest possible price, but to provide the necessary volume and cost/yield ratios the two countries had to engage in a complicated dance of supply and demand that terminated in a tasteless tomato, a shiny, red 'water bomb' that, in the end, no one wanted.[5]

Commercial cultivation has of course been transformed. Combined with massive international trade, it means we now have access to the summer fruit all year long wherever we live in the world, whether grown under glass, plastic or poly-ethylene, and whether by artificial light and heat or under the sun in another hemisphere. Greenhouse techniques are highly sophisticated: bumble-bees assure pollination, and wasps and ladybirds eat aphids; rockwool or perlite is the planting medium for hydroponic-grown tomatoes using computer-controlled irrigation and nutrient systems; tomato vines tower upwards as if in a tropical jungle; workers travel down the distant rows on mobile platforms and tramlines of pipes. It is what Mark Harvey, Steve Quilley and Huw Beynon call the 'fabrication of nature', at once both natural and artificial.[6]

Although natural sunshine may intuitively seem best when growing crops, in environmental protection terms the following should also be taken into account when it comes to greenhouse growing: improvements in energy use when heating glasshouses; the almost complete elimination of pesticide use (at least in the UK); major reductions in the use of fertilizers and their loss into the environment; highly efficient use of water; substitution for imports with their associated 'food miles' and lower environmental production standards. Not to mention the fact that even in Spain the sun does not always shine and most crops are now grown under polythene covers that need frequent replacement. Combined Heat and Power (CHP) schemes involve the siting of electricity-generating stations on tomato nurseries and have helped reduce CO_2 emissions; some growers are now using renewable

Hydroponic tomatoes (grown without soil in a water-based, nutrient-rich solution in which the roots may be supported by a medium such as perlite, gravel or, as in this case, coconut fibre).

Aeroponic tomatoes and lettuces: the roots hang in the air and are sprayed with a nutrient-rich mist.

energy sources to heat their greenhouses, such as straw or wood chips.[7]

The use of light has also become much more efficient when it comes to growing under glass in order to improve the rate of photosynthesis. Growers are exploring whether diffuse light rather than direct, for example, along with the use of LED lights, improve yields and vitamin C content. In the Netherlands energy saving is an important aim for the next decade, alongside reducing greenhouse gas emissions, water and land use.[8]

Natural greenhouse soils have to be replaced at frequent intervals or maintained from year to year by adding large quantities of fertilizers. In the USA interest in the possible use of complete nutrient solutions first began to develop around 1925. Hydroponics is now a versatile technology that can efficiently generate food crops from barren desert sand and desalinated ocean water, in mountainous regions too steep

Aquaponics combines conventional aquaculture (the raising of fish and other organisms) with hydroponics (soil-less growing) in an integrated system.

to farm, on city rooftops and concrete schoolyards and in arctic communities. In highly populated tourist areas where skyrocketing land prices have driven out traditional agriculture, hydroponics and aeroponics are providing locally grown high-value speciality crops such as fresh salad greens, herbs and cut flowers.[9] Except for organic growers, there is relatively little commercial tomato production in Europe and North America today directly in the soil.

The Living Box, for example, is an Israeli start-up that aims to enable Beduin families to grow fresh vegetables in the harsh, arid conditions of the Negev desert. They have developed a compact hydroponic kit that can be mass-produced, sold at a low price and easily operated by people with no agricultural training. The firm operates a commercial hydroponic greenhouse on the top of Tel Aviv's main shopping mall that supplies salad greens to many of the city's restaurants and food stores.[10]

New York-based Brightfarms is building aquaponic farms and greenhouses in urban settings. The company has partnered with over a dozen major retailers in the northeast and Midwest to sell produce grown within a 32 km (20-mi.) radius – with an eye on building greenhouses on the supermarkets' own roofs. There are initiatives in Bangladesh where saltwater has shrunk arable land to grow produce in vertical containers. In 2011 O'Hare Airport in Chicago installed the world's first aeroponic airport garden that provides vegetables, salad leaves and herbs for many of their restaurants, suspended in 26 towers that house over 1,100 planting spots. At the end of 2018, construction began at Dubai's Al Maktoum Airport of the world's largest vertical farm, with water use down to

Tomatoes growing at Lufa Farms, the world's first commercial rooftop greenhouse, in Montreal.

1 per cent of that used in conventional farming, provided by a closed-loop recycled system.[11]

The optimism these projects generate, however, needs an injection of scepticism, according to Paul West, a researcher in food security and sustainability at the University of Minnesota: 'Even if you put a greenhouse on every roof in every city in the world, it would still be too small a surface to feed the planet.'[12]

One of the most important issues in tomato growing is the need to cope with excessively hot or cold environments, too much water or too little, soil salinity or alkalinity. In dry or non-irrigated farming, the tomatoes are not watered after transplanting. This forces the roots to grow deep as they seek out moisture from winter water, thus producing more 'concentrated flavour'. Only certain cultivars, however, are suitable for this method, which works best in areas characterized by a cool wet season followed by a dry one. Yields may be low in 'dry' years, but the compensation can be exceptional flavour.

Some remarkable results have been reported from organic producer Pascal Poot, who farms in the dry and rocky Hérault region of France. His approach is to look after the soil but not the plants, which he encourages to fend for themselves. He has preserved many varieties of seeds and uses an ancient technique of 'warm layering' that involves placing last year's seeds into layers of decomposing manure in a greenhouse, then leaving them for several days until they germinate before they are planted out – and then ignored. He claims he is able to farm around four hundred varieties of organic tomatoes without watering, fertilizers, pesticides or even pastoral care. Ironically, many of his seeds are deemed 'illegal' as they are not entered in the Official Catalogue of Varieties of Vegetable Species, a situation he puts down to the monopolization of seed banks by multinational companies.[13]

Desert or arid-zone agriculture aims to increase productivity in such regions. In Spain, many coastal tomato growers have traditionally moved part of their production further inland in mid-summer to cooler areas. An ambitious European project (TomGEM) is seeking to develop varieties that are resistant to heat and can be grown cost-effectively in areas such as Valencia in Spain through July and August. At the other end of the spectrum, 2016 saw the first harvest from geothermal greenhouses in Van, eastern Turkey, where temperatures can drop to -46°C.[14]

Harnessing the sea and sun are seen by many as the way forward. The use of solar power to desalinate seawater for irrigation and provide energy offers good news for countries where an arid climate make them ill-equipped to meet the food needs of their growing populations. The concept was originally developed by Charlie Paton of Seawater Greenhouse Ltd in the UK, an award-winning company that has now carried out schemes in Tenerife, Abu Dhabi, Oman, Australia and Somaliland. The firm's former partner Sundrop Farms, based in the desert near the Australian city of Port Augusta, has taken a somewhat different technological route to achieve the same end with ongoing projects in Odemira in Portugal and Tennessee in the USA.

Our cultivated tomato has come a long way from the fields and markets of Aztec Tenochtitlan.

Tomato Picking

In the nineteenth century the new transcontinental railroads in the USA enabled the shipping of fresh produce from coast to coast and northwards from Florida to Chicago. New Jersey tomatoes had become that state's most profitable crop, but there were labour problems. On the large farms the pickers were African Americans; some canneries hired only women, often segregated by colour. After the intense summer harvest season, there was little other work for them.[15] However, it was California that was to dominate the processed tomato industry, employing thousands of low-wage ethnic workers, particularly Mexican *braceros*.

Nationwide farm labour shortages began during the Second World War and continued for decades. As tomatoes are a highly labour-intensive crop, the industry was among the hardest hit: the situation in California and Florida was especially acute, particularly as these states continued to plan expanded tomato production. However, compared to Midwestern and mid-Atlantic growers, California and Florida growers benefited from close proximity to migrant labour and also proved more adept at lobbying the federal government to allow migrant workers to work the harvest.[16]

Labour shortages can easily ruin an entire crop: in most cases the difference between a successful harvest and a complete failure is a matter of weeks. By the late 1950s, however, criticism of the migrant workers' scheme was mounting, most notably by American labour leaders who argued its continued existence undermined wage levels in agricultural and industrial sectors.

Without Mexican migrant labour the Californian tomato industry was doomed. Enter the mechanical tomato harvester. Two scientists at the University of California, Davis were to revolutionize tomato agriculture with their joint inventions of a mechanical tomato picker (later followed by an electronic sorter) and a hybrid tomato that could be picked by a metal grip without damaging the fruit.[17] Starting in the 1940s, over the next twenty years their aim was to develop a tomato with four key qualities: uniform ripening, a smaller plant with fewer tomatoes, and fruit which could come off the vine readily but not too easily and was sturdy enough to be handled in this way.

At first there was little interest from the industry, particularly at a cost of $25,000 for each machine. However, when the federal government decided to crack down on the *braceros*, it set off a panic. Many farmers abandoned their farms, leaving the remaining growers to consolidate and mechanize.[18]

In Florida, the home of the fresh, out-of-season tomato, growers began looking into mechanizing their production in the 1960s as imports from Cuba and Mexico threatened to undermine their markets. Although fresh tomatoes were more fragile than those destined for canning, the farmers created massive 'factories in the field' to make sorting and harvesting more efficient. They could not eliminate the need for large amounts of labour, but they did reduce some of the costs thanks to protective trade policies and tariffs from the federal government.[19] Labour costs are still estimated as being between 30 and 50 per cent of greenhouse production costs. MetoMotion is an Israeli start-up developing a multi-purpose robotic harvesting system for high-tech greenhouses that will also generate data on the crop such as plant stress and yield. It also plans to incorporate pruning, monitoring, pollination and de-leafing.[20]

Nonetheless, it will be a long time before manual labour becomes redundant, and there are still regular reports of horrific scandals involving the effect of illegally sprayed chemicals on pickers, and a form of labour imprisonment in which undocumented immigrants are kept under lock and key and forced to give up large parts of their wages. Immokalee in Florida has been described as 'ground zero for modern day slavery'. In addition, some years ago, a shocking number of babies were born with severe deformities after their mothers were exposed to pesticides while harvesting tomatoes.[21]

In 2001 the Coalition of Immokalee Workers (CIW) launched a boycott of Taco Bell (owned by Yum! Brands, a huge chain that also controls Pizza Hut, KFC, A&W and Long John Silver's). By 2004 the protest against the 'sweat shops in the fields' culminated in a massive demonstration and ten-day hunger strike outside Taco Bell headquarters in California. Soon after, Yum! agreed to the coalition's request for wages to rise one penny more per pound, a pittance for huge corporations but the difference between a below-poverty and paltry wage for a picker. McDonald's followed two years later but Burger King, Subway and Whole Foods, supported by the Tomato Growers Exchange, held out until 2008. Only the growers refused to participate, even though the pay increase would be at no direct cost to them.

It took two further years of bad publicity, legal wrangling, catastrophic freezes, collapse in tomato prices and competition from greenhouse and hydroponic producers in Canada and Mexico as well as the USA before there was widespread agreement in 2010 on a 'Fair Food Code of Conduct'.[22] This unique, progressive legislation both increased pay (although many farmworkers still earn below the poverty line) and was intended to establish legally binding mechanisms to defend human, social and labour rights. Unfortunately, further protests broke out in 2015 when Wendy's, a huge burger chain that has always refused to sign up to the Code, shifted its sourcing to Mexico, where workers have few protections. There were further protests in 2018, but Wendy's continues to claim that the purchasing decision was based on the better quality of the tomatoes, not the Fair Food Program.[23]

Exploitation has not been restricted to North America. In Europe a vast, shimmering 'sea of plastic' polytunnels in Almeria, Spain (the 'costa del polythene') – which boasts a two-billion-euro-a-year tomato industry – has been (and often still is) the workplace for thousands of poorly paid labourers from Morocco, West Africa and Romania. Living in shanty towns, they are at the bottom of a pressurized food chain dominated by multinational supermarkets.

As migrants come to Italy in rising numbers, more and more are also swept into the illegal tomato picking industry, and held in slave-like conditions by unaccountable work-gang masters in rural ghettos.[24] A research project by the Ethical Trading Initiative (ETI) alliance of companies, trade unions and NGOs, released in December 2015, described a mobile, seasonal workforce living in extreme poverty, often without water and sanitation, housed in abandoned buildings or tent cities with little or no healthcare.[25]

The tomato is a taste of history, but too often it comes at a cost the consumer willingly ignores. It is, one might say, the 'inhuman' tomato.

Vine-ripened tomatoes in Spain.

8
Varieties, Organics and Heirlooms

On its arrival in Europe several centuries earlier, the tomato continued to be improved. Indeed, its very existence in Europe brought an unexpected benefit, as most wild tomato stock required halictus bees for pollination. These were not present in the Mediterranean regions, so only the rarer self-pollinating tomatoes survived. Thus, unintentionally, European botanists and gardeners were more easily able to replicate tomato plants with desirable traits through seed selection.[1]

The botanical qualities of the tomato have enabled it to grow relatively easily in different soils and climatic conditions, and it can even spring up in weed patches and wild ground. Depending on the variety, it can grow and fruit rapidly and be relatively easily harvested (at least compared with digging up potatoes). Andrew F. Smith quotes the New Jersey *Morris County Whig*, which asserted in the nineteenth century that there was no vegetable that could be 'cultivated with less care and trouble, and none which will, if properly treated, yield in greater abundance'.

One great step forward occurred when Dr T. J. Hand of New York crossed cherry tomatoes with the more commonly grown lumpy, large ones to produce Trophy, a variety of tomato with 'a solid mass of flesh and juice, small seeds and

A sign commemorating Alexander Livingston in Reynoldsburg, Ohio.

REYNOLDSBURG-
BIRTHPLACE OF THE TOMATO

Alexander W. Livingston, plant breeder, horticulturist and seed merchant, who became internationally known through his development of the tomato, was born October 14, 1821, the son of John and Mary Graham Livingston. The first known variety of the tomato was the Paragon produced by Livingston by selection and crossing in a field of many varieties on his "Buckeye Farm" located at 1792 Graham Road, City of Reynoldsburg, Franklin County, Ohio. Livingston died November 11, 1898 and is buried in Greenlawn Cemetery, Columbus, Ohio.

smooth skin' that had 'unbounded success' after the Civil War.[2] More significant still was the work of Alexander Livingston, described by tomato expert Craig LeHoullier as 'the world's most creative tomato-breeding mind in the late 1800s'. He introduced many major varieties, including the smooth-skinned Paragon and Acme, but perhaps his greatest contribution was to understand how different tomatoes could be developed for different market needs.[3]

Commercial hybrids were created by intentionally cross-pollinating two different tomato varieties with the aim of producing an offspring containing the best traits of each, such as early ripening or smooth skin. However, because they are a cross, their seed will not grow true, which means farmers cannot save them for use in following years and have to buy new seeds each growing season.

Nonetheless, the advantages of reliability, uniformity, consistency and (often) disease resistance over true breeding varieties were so great that growers were willing to buy these seeds at higher prices. LeHoullier notes that seeds saved from hybrids will produce tomatoes – but what type of tomato results is another matter and for the average home gardener it may not be worth the space and effort involved.[4]

In 1946 the first hybrid tomato cultivar, Single Cross, was released, but it was Big Boy – released by Burpee in 1949 – that was to revolutionize the tomato-breeding industry with its impact on size and yield: large, smooth, round, red tomatoes were now the commercial (and consumer) archetype. LeHoullier describes it as a part of Americana following the end of the Second World War that, in a way, defined the Victory Garden.[5]

As agribusiness grew alongside the use of synthetic fertilizers, so did hybrid cultivars for both the fresh and processed markets. In the second part of the century, breeding had various aims: increased yield, long shelf life, nutritional value and more while holding production costs as low as possible. Taste has not always been a high priority.

In Florida, which caters predominantly for the fast-food industry, this has meant providing big, firm tomatoes that can be sliced to the precise millimetre to fit neatly on a burger. They are bred to be sturdy and thick-skinned enough for long-distance transportation, multiple handling and extended refrigeration for year-round availability. The disadvantage of both chilling and gassing is the prevention of natural flavour development, but there is an over-riding supermarket and food service demand for tomatoes that are consistently round, smooth, even and scarlet-hued. They are hard, as well: throw a tomato at a politician these days and it won't squish, simply stun.

A relatively new commercial selling point is 'vine-ripened', a sales gimmick that trades on the belief that the tomato looks more natural when attached to the vine and smells as tomatoes are supposed to smell. The fruit is simply cut off the plant when 'mature green', or at a point when the fruit will continue to mature and redden even after it is picked. It then ripens in the same way as loose ones unattached to the plant, despite the fact it is usually sold at a premium. Although cultivars are important, the USP is the aroma from the calyx and truss.

The concept of the 'snacking' tomato has become a huge industry driver, aimed at consumers on the go.[6] Almost all come from high-tech, hydroponic greenhouses, but because they are protected while growing and handled more gently during packing and shipping, they can be bred for flavour and picked when ripe. The small, crunchy SanLucar praline tomato, grown in a Tunisian oasis, stands out for quality due to many hours of sunshine, particularly fertile soil and mineral water from a nearby thermal spring.

Cultivars have been developed for many purposes from greenhouse cultivation to growing outdoors in short, cool summers of regions such as Siberia. Many commercial plants have fruit that ripen at the same time, which can allow for mechanical harvesting and fast picking. Specific sizes and types are grown especially for processing, whether the end result is whole canned, crushed, diced or dried tomatoes, juice, sauce, paste or purée. These varieties generally remain on the vine until both colour and flavouring develop, which is one reason canned tomatoes tend to be superior in winter and spring to fresh commercial ones.

Research for new varieties is highly competitive and the pressure has produced some intriguing results. A researcher for Syngenta in France has been developing a honey-coloured tomato that does not rot but slowly becomes candied, rather like a date, and tastes like jam.[7] In Australia specialist supplier Abundant Produce has cross-bred hybrid seeds to produce tough tomatoes that can survive temperatures of 50 degrees Celsius (122°F) and have been successfully tested in the hot Punjab province of Pakistan.[8]

Ironically, despite all the super-advanced technology, actually making the seed itself remains a labour-intensive business as each tomato plant must be hand-pollinated (as opposed to open pollination) and is mostly done in countries with low labour costs such as India, Chile, Thailand, China and Taiwan. By contrast, more community-orientated seed banks such as the Open Source Seed Initiative (OSSI), inspired by the open source software movement, campaign to 'free the seeds'

Tomato production in China, using bamboo frames.

locked away from use by intellectual property rights and restrictive corporate patents.

On the other side of the globe, China has become a major force in world tomato production for processing, although it is only in the last hundred years that the tomato has been integrated into the Chinese kitchen. Tomato paste is for them a valuable trade commodity and so much cheap paste was shipped to Italy in 2005 that Italian tomatoes were left to rot in the fields. There have also been earlier scandals of customs agents in Italy seizing tons of rotting, worm-infested Chinese paste. European and Californian paste may be superior for now but it may only be a matter of time before they face competition on both the quality and cost fronts.[9]

Organics

Although they don't top the list, tomatoes feature regularly in the *'Dirty Dozen' Shopper's Guide to Pesticides in Produce* produced by the respected u.s. Environmental Working Group (EWG).[10] At certain times of the year, 90 per cent of fresh u.s. tomatoes are grown in Florida, but as Barry Estabrook points out, the state is about the worst possible place in which to grow tomatoes. Both the climate and the sandy soil are completely unsuitable, so farmers must drench their fields in chemicals to have any hope of a crop. In addition Florida's humidity breeds large populations of insects, which means tomato growers need to apply pesticides on a weekly basis. In *Tomatoland* he calls it not the 'Sunshine State' but the 'Pesticide State'.[11]

It is a rather different story in the UK where few, if any, pesticides are used on British-grown tomato crops, a huge improvement over the last decade. Growers here were among the first to use natural enemies of pests, rather than chemical sprays, as a control method although when alien pests turn up it is always a reminder of the need for fully integrated management systems.[12]

There are many reasons for the rise of organic agriculture, especially as a reaction against the perceived excesses of agri-business. Past and present concerns include the overuse of chemical pesticides and fertilizers, lack of crop rotation and the cultivation of foods for maximum profit rather than taste and nutritional value. Not all industrial food is necessarily evil but for many people concerns over labour rights and abuses provide another reason to turn to alternative tomato sourcing (on the basis that exploitation of workers is less likely to happen in an organic, ethically aspirational environment).

Issues concerning food health and safety and rising prices have also motivated a revival of home gardening, allotments and community gardens. After describing the neat rows and perfect-looking fruits produced by industrial agriculture, Tim Stark said of his own harvests:

> The eye for smooth-sailing symmetry ran aground at my renegade tomatoes, chilies and eggplants. Planted by hand and never abetted by herbicide, my rows were woefully crooked, and lost in a sea of run-amok weeds.[13]

It was nonetheless a proud and defiant rebellion that defined foodie culture while pushing a broader spectrum of consumers towards an appreciation of the fresh, the homemade, the local and natural via the conduit of value-for-money farmers' markets. Many urban gardeners can also now grow food inside their homes, as a host of products from self-watering potted tomato plants to full-on artificially lit hydroponic systems have come on the market.[14]

Heirlooms

The other side of the coin to futuristic hybrids is the growth of interest in 'heirloom' or 'heritage' tomatoes. There are thousands of varieties that have been identified as heirlooms, generally meaning they have existed for at least fifty years and are open-pollinated: fertilized by insects, wind and other natural means. The seeds that result can be saved and, through selection, improved over time.

According to Craig LeHoullier, heirloom or heritage tomatoes have history and value, but the term itself is somewhat vague and there is no clear age at which a vegetable is considered an heirloom. He defines two categories: true family heirlooms and the non-hybrid, pre-1950 varieties such as the delicious Golden Queen that Livingston described as a 'very pretty yellow tomato'. Thanks to the work of LeHoullier and friends, the Golden Queen is among three heirlooms (including Favorite and Magnus) that originated from Livingston and have been brought back to life by utilizing the tomato-seed collection in the Germplasm Resources Information Network (GRIN) database at the U.S. Department of Agriculture.

The trend reflects an increasing concern for sustainability, genetic diversity and flavour choice and, thanks to the dedication of various seed collectors, not all old varieties have been consigned to oblivion. Jennifer A. Jordan in *Edible Memory* points out that biodiversity is not just about flavour and looks or its adoption as a badge of an elite lifestyle. It is also about invisible traits such as resistance to disease or adverse conditions that may be able to help us globally in the face of future environmental challenges. However, she also explains that it is difficult to calculate how much agricultural biodiversity has been lost, in part because of similarities between varieties, in part because of name changes and because few systematic records have been kept.

Heritage tomatoes and those protected by the EU DOP/IGP legislation overlap but are not necessarily the same. Protection has been given in Europe to the San Marzano, the Pomodorino del piennolo del Vesuvio and the Sicilian Pachino, and Slow Food recognizes several others in its Presidia section, such as the Kurtovo Konare pink tomato from Bulgaria and the rare Siccagno tomato from the Bilìci Valley in Sicily, which is particularly good for paste or 'triple extract'. The Slow Food Ark of Taste includes varieties such as the Basque bunch tomatoes from Busturia, and the Platense tomato brought to Brazil by Spanish, Portuguese and Italian immigrants in the 1930s. A good candidate for inclusion would be the juicy, Catalan 'hanging' tomatoes from Más dels Fumeros, grown on canes in open ground and strung on rope and which can last for months without refrigeration.[15]

Canned tomatoes are rarely identified by variety, but the San Marzano is an exception. It has attained almost cult-like status on gourmet tables but the narrow, elongated fruit is often cloaked in a cloud of misunderstanding. It is not an ancient pure-blood breed but a cross between the Re Umberto and Fiaschetto varieties, and first came to prominence in the early twentieth century. Its bittersweet flavour, thick flesh, minimal core and low moisture content make it excellent for canning or sauce-making.

San Marzano or San Marzano-style tomato varieties can be grown anywhere but only those produced in the EU-approved Italian region around Mount Vesuvius in Campania (and that also meet other production criteria) are eligible for DOP certification and are allowed on the true Neapolitan pizza. Demand, however, outstrips supply and unfortunately, there is some reason to believe that quality and yield have been adversely affected as a result of industrial pollution in the area.[16] The marketplace is notoriously rife with falsely labelled cans selling at premium prices. Little wonder the San Marzano has been called the fake Rolex of canned foods.

When blight struck the variety in the 1970s, it forced canning companies to produce more disease-resistant and sturdier hybrids such as the USDA-bred Roma. These can be good but they are not pure in the sense sought by heirloom-seekers. Twenty years later several companies tried to recapture the genetic code of the virtually lost original San Marzano tomato and produced the Cirio Selection 3 and the SMEC-20. The latter cultivar is the closest to the original ecotype and is grown by Sabato Abagnale. Controversially, he does not remove the skins in his Miracle of San Gennaro brand as required by DOP regulations. However, the fine, flavour-bearing skin dissolves during cooking, amalgamating with the pulp. Hand-picked only in the evening when very ripe, they really are the tinned-tomato-lover's tomato.

Some heirlooms are 'gnarly looking, old-fashioned tomatoes, the kind Grandpa and Great-Grandpa grew', and for many gardeners their revival has become a lifelong passion. Ken Whealy, for example, after planting a few seeds from a Bavarian relative, ultimately started an extensive organization, the Seed Saver's Exchange, devoted to the saving and swapping of heirloom vegetable seeds.[17]

If nothing else, their wonderful names tell stories that reflect history, culture, personal experience and whimsy. Mortgage Lifter, for example, enabled its creator in the 1930s to pay off his $6,000 mortgage in six years. Abraham Lincoln was originally advertised in 1923 as 'The Giant of all Tomatoes', along with a portrait of the president. Brandywine produced for LeHoullier a 'perfect tomato-eating experience' with flavours that explode in the mouth.

In the UK noted heritage varieties include Ailsa Craig, which is thought to have originated around 1908 near Inverness, Scotland. Christopher Stocks describes it as one of the main so-called 'Scotch Tomatoes' that ripened early in a mild, localized microclimate, providing its growers with a useful competitive advantage. Carter's Golden Sunrise has a fabulous, rich and sweet flavour and has won hands down in taste trials of traditional versus modern varieties held by the National Trust.[18]

Not every heritage tomato has the flavour of lost times that matches the seductive memory of how we think they used to taste. When food writer Frank Bruni despairingly described in the *New York Times* how 'a thousand heirloom tomato salads bloomed' it wincingly hit home. Heirloom tomatoes can be delicious, but they can also be underwhelming, an overpriced fad and marketing tool. The excessively hyped fashion for heirlooms, however, does not diminish their botanical and cultural value. And while many hybrids are undoubtedly bland

San Marzano tomatoes.

Page from the *Johnson & Stokes Garden and Farm Manual* of 1890 showing Brandywine tomatoes.

or watery, or have the texture of cotton wool, there are plenty of exceptions: Sun Gold cherry tomatoes, for example, are as sweet as candy with an addictive snap.

The marriage of heirlooms with hybrids to make a progeny that combines attractive appearance and taste with good production and disease resistance is a way forward. The Traditom European project aims at recovering historic tomato varieties typical of the Mediterranean basin by creating hybrids with the shape, size, colour and flavour of the past. Under their auspices in 2017, Meridiem Seeds introduced a highly promising new type of Marmande tomato – deep-green, large, ribbed and shiny.[19] And another excellent cross has now appeared on the market: the Spanish Monterosa. Asymmetrical, flattened and ribbed, it is a cross between the Girona pear tomato, DO, and the Italian Costoluto Genoveso. Heirbrid or hyloom, it's good news for tomato-lovers everywhere.

The laboratory, however, has not always produced such happy results. The spectre of GM still hangs over the tomato world.

9
Science and Technology

Tomatoes have always stimulated fundamental questions about science, technology and markets and the many ways in which human behaviour interacts with nature. The history of the tomato impacts directly on social, political and economic forces – and vice-versa.

GM and Molecular Breeding

Tomatoes were the world's first genetically modified whole food. Tomato scientists initially broke new ground by altering the plant in order to change its nutritional quality as a foodstuff and its health-giving properties, rather than to increase yield as with soya, corn and cotton. As such, the scientists' work was focused on the consumer rather than the producer.

The advent of the Flavr Savr tomato was intended as a game-changer. In 1994 it was engineered to suppress the ripening gene so it would remain firm after harvesting, thus offering a great advantage to the producer and distributor. In the UK modified tomatoes appeared in processed form as cans of purée in 1996.

Cans of American tomato purée made from genetically modified tomatoes.

Neither the Flavr Savr nor the purée lasted on the market longer than two years, and the pursuit of a lycopene-enhanced tomato was put on indefinite hold. This was brought about by consumer resistance, a loss of confidence in food and science following a sequence of public health shocks, development costs, poor yield of the tomatoes in question, patenting issues and the alliance of radical ecologists and agricultural traditionalists in the 'defence of Nature'.

Over the next two decades the situation changed. Traditional cross-breeding can be lengthy and unreliable, reliant on a lot of serendipity, but modern hybridization techniques have been transformed by major advances in molecular biology and marker-assisted DNA sequences. It is a long way from the Flavr Savr.

It is, in fact, a biotechnology that is generally well-regarded by industry and NGOs alike. As the authors of *Exploring the Tomato* write,

> So long as genetic material is passed from one plant to another by means of sexual reproduction, rather than by direct insertion into the germ cell, there is hybridisation and not 'engineering' or 'modification'. The difference is in the means by which a DNA sequence finds its way into the plant.[1]

Norfolk Plant Sciences Ltd in the UK have developed genetically modified purple-fleshed tomatoes by transferring genes from two other plant species that contain the high levels of anti-oxidants and anthocyanin normally found in fruits such as blueberries and blackberries.[2] One of the main problems, however, is that while looking for genetic markers in individual plants may be getting cheaper all the time, generating enormous quantities of seed and marketing it to farmers is still costly and thus dominated by giant seed companies rather than public institutions: they have the resources and can develop some good finished varieties, but the price is that they also control the germplasm and technology.[3]

Marker-assisted selection, however, can have a darker side when put in the context of biopiracy.

From the Wild to the Lab

Despite the Technicolor array of tomatoes on show at many farmers' markets, both hybrid and heirloom tomatoes are, genetically speaking, remarkably similar. They may be diverse when it comes to shape, size and colour but all that variety is literally only skin deep. As a consequence of inbreeding during domestication, the genetic diversity in cultivated tomatoes is very narrow; it is estimated they possess only around 5 per cent of the total variation present within the primitive varieties that are native to Peru and Ecuador.

Wild tomatoes often display valuable qualities – disease resistance; lack of seeds; higher yields; improved composition and colour of fruit; and cold, drought and salt tolerance – and can pass on these traits when crossed with commercial varieties. DNA hybridization technology now allows traits from the natural gene pool to be bred back into cultivated species and in order to benefit from these untapped genes, biotechnology companies have looked to tomatoes' original home, the Andes, in a strange historical loop that brings together the ultra-modern with pre-civilization.

Most wild tomatoes are found in narrow geographical regions and have very small populations, making them vulnerable to extinction. Unfortunately, time may be running out as a result of the incursion of modern agricultural practices from bulldozing to logging. Ranching and blasting with herbicide along with roadbuilding and urban sprawl also eliminate habitat for wild tomatoes: herds of goats, llamas, alpacas and other domestic animals eat and trample them. Even though the prestigious C. M. Rick Tomato Genetics Resource Center at the University of California, Davis, can preserve a certain amount of seeds and plants, such collections are no substitute for gathering those in situ, meaning ones that grow in their native environments without human interference.

Additionally, apart from the increasing spectre of species destruction and loss of biodiversity, plant and seed-gathering has become the focus of patent claims between the countries of origin, particularly Peru and Ecuador, and multinational corporations and universities. The tomato has become a political hot potato.

Beginning in 1992, members of the United Nations approved a treaty called the Convention on Biological Diversity. It established international regulations on the exploitation of genetic resources, including seeds and plants. If researchers from one nation want to use biological resources from another nation, they must first get the latter's consent and fully inform the donor country about what they plan to do with the material. A corporation or university that profits from use of the biological resources must share the money equitably with the country of origin.

Every single member of the UN apart from the United States ratified the treaty. The procedure has its critics: negotiations with the countries of origin can be extremely complex, bureaucratic and time-consuming. On the other hand there are great legal and political challenges as complicated arguments about patenting, 'seed piracy' and benefit-sharing work their way through the international arena.

Large agrochemical corporations and institutions argue that the results are new inventions so can be patented. Opponents describe this as 'theft' of a nation's patrimony and a privatization of the tomato genome, as the plant and seeds may have been taken or used without appropriate authorization. Examples include the Swiss Syngenta patent application for firmer tomatoes (a desirable trait in industrial farming), as identified in the Peruvian native *Solanum pennellii*; the American company Evolutionary Genomics, which has laid claim to two genes identified in a wild tomato species endemic to the Galápagos Islands that relate to salt and drought-tolerance in one, and extra sweetness in the other; and Israeli government researchers who have filed for a patent on a gene originating in Peru that encodes resistance to the devastating tomato yellow leaf curl virus transmitted by whitefly.[4]

Scientists at the University of Florida hit the headlines in 2017 when they were hailed as restoring flavour to the mass-market tomato bred for quantity over quality. Partially funded by Monsanto, they researched older varieties of tomato in order to identify and understand the volatile aromatic compounds that interplay with sugars and acids to determine flavour. The problem was that a lot of old cultivars go soft quickly, have skin that cracks and scars easily, and come from low-yielding plants. The scientists' aim was to produce a high-yield, supermarket-ready tomato with the taste and looks of an heirloom. When the university released two of these hybrids, Garden Gem and Garden Treasure, they were hailed as the best of both tomato worlds.[5]

The open-pollinated, heirloom 'parents', however, are not subject to restrictive intellectual property claims, and are often freely released and exchanged by public breeding programmes. So, according to critics, the question is whether patent applications will reveal the geographical pedigree used in the new varieties. As their fierce opponent Edward Hammond charged, twenty-first-century American university scientists had exploited the chemistry and genetic resources of traditional varieties developed by indigenous peoples, farmers and breeders:

> Florida researchers might be proud of the scientific accomplishment of the more chemically-detailed understanding of tomato taste that they have developed, but they should be ashamed to have claimed the use and manipulation of tomato volatile flavors, in both breeding and in foods, as something they hve invented and own.[6]

Technology for the Future

There is now scarcely a country where tomatoes are not grown. China tops the list as the largest producer (at least for processed tomatoes), followed by India, the u.s. and Turkey, and scientists continue to push the boundaries of cultivation along with increased environmental awareness.

The tomato's natural need for rest, its circadian rhythm, for example, has been altered by Dutch geneticists using a trait from wild tomatoes that deals with light. A full 24-hour growth cycle of the tomato that never sleeps, using continuous light, can result in a huge increase in crop productivity.[7] In Turkey, researchers are working on a variety that can actually become more tasty under stress conditions such as drought or increased salt levels from irrigation or fertilization.[8] Scientists in the usa have been developing a 'tomato battery' that would turn rotten, damaged and generally unfit-for-sale tomatoes into electricity. This would provide green energy as well as tackling the large-scale tomato waste problem in which vast quantities are dumped into landfills and waterways each year, especially in Florida.[9]

In the processing world it may come as a surprise to find how much water is needed in order to peel fruit for canning: a 28-ounce (830-ml) can, for example, requires 27 ounces of water to remove the skin. To cope with drought years, researchers at uc Davis have developed a way to blanch and peel fruit with infrared rays.

The large quantity of tomato seeds produced during the industrial processing of sauce are usually considered waste by the food industry, but Spanish researchers have recently identified a key gene in the production of seedless tomato fruits, a potential advantage in increasing shelf life and in the manufacture of juices and pastes.[10] Seeds, though, have an

A food research scientist injects a tomato to both enrich taste and improve resistance to parasites and cold temperatures.

overlooked environmental potential, and tomato seed oil has a possible use as a biodiesel and renewable source of energy. Waste left over from ketchup is the subject of a joint project between Heinz and the Ford Motor Company to develop a new type of plastic.[11] By contrast, in 2017 a Spanish study identified a key gene in the production of seedless tomato fruits – something that could increase shelf life and expedite the manufacture of juices and pastes.[12]

Innovative packaging is another growth area: a solid cardboard box enriched with tomato plant fibres produced by Solidus Solutions was declared the winner of the Packaging Europe Sustainability Awards 2016.[13] A French company has also developed cardboard packaging made from the recycled stems and leaves of the plants, which are then used as containers for the tomatoes themselves, an innovation adapted by the British supermarket chain Waitrose in 2018.[14]

In 2014 award-winning researchers at the John Innes Centre in the UK launched their new biotech company, Persephone Bio Ltd, with the aim of using biotechnology to manufacture sought-after bioactive ingredients from modified fruit such as tomatoes and oranges for the cosmetics industry, as well as therapeutic ones to treat skin conditions or promote wound healing.[15] In Iceland, the Friðheimar farm and restaurant grow and serve tomatoes year-round in a greenhouse using geothermal energy. This is a small-scale operation, but the German Aerospace Centre (DLR) had a bigger ambition when they announced in September 2018 a successful vegetable harvest in an Antarctic greenhouse (EDEN ISS) that reproduced Mars-like conditions.[16] The following month the German research satellite Eu:CROPIS, with a cargo of 24 tomato seeds, left Bremen for California, where it was due to be launched into space. The aim is to create a breathable atmosphere and food for astronaut missions lasting several years using an automated system to provide the tomatoes with water, fertilizer and light.[17]

The extraordinary story of the 'human tomato' continues.

Recipes

But now that whole fields of the vegetable are in cultivation all over the country, the cookery books give many recipes dealing with it, most of them, unfortunately, erring grievously on the side of elaboration. Like the oyster, the tomato has a natural flavour so distinctive and so delicious, that anything beyond the simplest cooking must rob it of some of its gustatory value. To stuff a tomato with mushrooms, as recommended in more than one recipe, is to prove oneself destitute of a refined and cultivated palate.

The Hotel World (December 1895)

Tomato Sauce, Spanish-style (1692)

Rudolf Grewe, 'The Arrival of the Tomato in Spain and Italy: Early Recipes', *Journal of Gastronomy*, iii/2 (1987)

Antonio Latini's sauce was made with finely chopped fresh tomato, onion and chillies and dressed with oil, salt and pepper. It is actually more of a condiment and bears a striking similarity to today's salsas:

> Take half a dozen tomatoes that are ripe, and put them to roast in the embers, and when they are scorched, remove the skin diligently, and mince them finely with a knife. Add onions, minced finely, to discretion; hot chilli peppers,

also minced finely; and thyme in a small amount. After mixing everything together, adjust it with a little salt, oil, and vinegar. It is a very tasty sauce, both for boiled dishes or anything else.

Haddock with Tomatoes
Juan Altamiras, *Nuevo arte de cocina* (1747)

Two eighteenth-century recipes. The first, by Altamiras, is surprisingly modern and relevant; Hannah Glasse's version is less appealing. An early English misinterpretation of how they thought the Spanish cooked, perhaps, all oil and garlic!

Fry onions and a lot of tomatoes; place the pieces of fish on the bottom of a wide pot and cover them with layers of tomato, parsley, pepper and crushed garlic . . . There is no need for any other spice as the tomato provides it all. It is a delicious dish and, later on in this book, I will teach you how to preserve tomatoes throughout the year.

To Dress Haddocks after the Spanish Way
Hannah Glasse, *The Art of Cookery, Made Plain And Easy* (1774)

Take a haddock, washed very clean and dried, and broil it nicely; then take a quarter of a pint of oil in a stew pan, season it with mace, cloves and nutmeg, pepper and salt, two cloves of garlick, some love apples when in season, a little vinegar; put in the fish, cover it close, and let it stew half an hour over a slow fire.

To Dress Lamb's Head and Feet (1824)

Mary Randolph in *The Virginia Housewife* broke new ground by including a number of recipes that featured tomatoes. As Andrew

F. Smith has said, 'She set the standards for tomato cookery for the next three decades.'[1] This recipe fits right in with the movement for nose-to-tail eating pioneered by British chef Fergus Henderson.

Clean them very nicely, and boil them till tender, take off the flesh from the head with the eyes, also mince the tongue and heart, which must be boiled with the head; split the feet in two, put them with the pieces from the head and the mince, into a pint of good gravy, seasoned with pepper, salt, and tomato catsup, or ripe tomatoes: stew it till tender, thicken the gravy, and lay the liver cut in slices and broiled over it – garnish with crisp parsley and bits of curled bacon.

Chelsea Sauce

In the film *Meet Me in St Louis*, a 1944 look at American life at the turn of the twentieth century, there is a kitchen scene where the household are in the final stages of making ketchup, arguing among themselves about the failings of the latest batch – too sour, too sweet, too flat – until, satisfied, they pour it into glass bottles. They were making a free-flowing liquid that was the norm until commercial producers set a standard that was thicker and smoother, with more sugar and vinegar than homemade varieties.

This is a recipe from *Good Housekeeping* magazine of May 1886, which the writer claimed was 'experimentally prepared and carefully tested' and superior to tomato catsup.

Twenty-four ripe tomatoes, eight onions, six peppers, eight coffee cups of good vinegar, eight tablespoons of sugar, eight spoonfuls of salt, one spoonful cinnamon, one tablespoon of allspice, one nutmeg, one spoonful of cloves. Boil all together well, and seal while hot.

Independence Day Salad (1904)

Christine Terhune Herrick, *Consolidated Library of Modern Cooking and Household Recipes – Book IV: Vegetables, Fruits and Cereals; Bread and Cakes; Salads and Relishes; Ices, Pastry, and Other Desserts* (New York, 1904)

In the early nineteenth century, tomatoes were mostly eaten cooked, often boiled for hours. The suspicion that the tomato was poisonous may have lingered on, though Christopher Stocks proposes an alternative explanation based on the uncertain purity of the water supply at the time: 'They were probably only doing what we would be advised to do today when travelling to less developed countries, where cooked food is reckoned to be safer than food that has simply been washed.'[2]

Half a century on and raw tomatoes were featuring in the salads that had become a mainstay on middle-class American tables. In 1905, home economist Christine Herrick ruled 'the salad is the prince of the menu, and though the dinner may be perfect in every detail, it is incomplete without a good salad.' Early forms of salads typically included only one primary ingredient – lettuce, cucumber or tomato, for example – and were usually dressed with oil or mayonnaise.

For those keen to prove their patriotism by preparing an Independence Day-themed salad, Herrick provided this recipe. Unable to find an appropriate blue-coloured ingredient, she opted instead for the use of a blue serving plate:

> Use the white hearts of lettuce, making the leaves into little nests on a blue platter or shallow bowl. Into each nest put a small round tomato, scalded and peeled, and then chilled. Garnished the edge with round red radishes, with the peeling cut into points and turned back to show the white. Pour over it a French dressing.

Poulette Creole: A Good Way of Cooking Chicken

A recipe from the *San Francisco Call*, December 1912 contributed by a Mrs Joe Denks. With a little adjustment, it would still work well today.

> Two very fine chickens, two tablespoons of butter, two tablespoons of flour, six fresh tomatoes, six fresh green peppers, two cloves of garlic, six large onions, three sprigs of thyme, parsley and two bay leaves, one pint of consommé, salt and pepper to taste.

Take the chickens and clean nicely and cut into pieces at the joints. Season well with salt and pepper. Put the butter in a saucepan and when it melts add the chicken. Let this brown slowly for about fifteen minutes. Have ready six large onions sliced; add these to the chicken and let them brown. Every inch must be nicely browned, but not in the slightest degree burned. Add two tablespoons of flour; let this brown. Then add half a dozen fresh tomatoes sliced and let these brown. Cook very slowly, allowing the mixture to simply simmer (do not let boil); add chopped parsley, thyme and bay leaves and two cloves of garlic finely minced. Let all brown without burning, cover and let simmer over a slow fire. The tomato juice will make sufficient gravy. Add half a dozen sweet peppers, take seeds out and slice very fine; stir well; let all simmer for twenty minutes at least; keep well-covered and stir often so it will not burn. After simmering for twenty minutes, add a cup of consommé. Let it cook again for about one hour very, very slowly, over a steady fire and season again to taste; cook a few minutes more and serve hot.

Tomato Omelette

A Calendar of Food and Wine by Nell Heaton and André Simon was published in 1949 in London. It had a chapter for each month, describing foods-in-season, notes on nature and poetry, and musings on wine. This November recipe is simple, comforting and ideal for a light lunch or supper in a month when the days seems to fly away so fast.

Blanch, skin and slice three tomatoes. Fry in melted butter and keep hot. Beat up two or three eggs, season with salt and pepper. Pour into a hot pan with sufficient melted butter to prevent the omelette catching. When set put tomatoes in centre, fold over, place on a dish and garnish with sprigs of watercress before serving.

Tomato Soup Spice Cake
(circa 1966, but timeless!)

Tomato soup cake has become an American dessert legend ever since it first appeared in community cookbooks in the 1920s and '30s. It reflects the frugality of Depression-era cooking and was sometimes called 'Mystery Cake' because of its secret ingredient. Spices enliven the basic cake mix and the tomato soup added moisture, rather than using milk, oil or other dairy products. Its popularity has endured ever since.

Campbell's Soup launched their own version in 1940, at first a British-style steamed pudding with very little fat. This evolved into a more cake-like product and as butter rationing was dropped, cake recipes became more lavish. The accompanying cream cheese frosting was a 1970s introduction but is now regarded as standard.

1 can condensed tomato soup (preferably Campbell's)
1 tsp bicarbonate of soda
180 g (1 cup) caster sugar
2 eggs
75 g (⅓ cup) butter plus extra for greasing
1 tsp ground cinnamon
½ tsp ground cloves
salt
200 g (1½ cups) plain flour
4 tsp baking powder
150 g (1 cup) raisins

230 g (one 8-oz package) cream cheese, softened
2 tbsp milk
1 tsp vanilla extract
500 g (4 cups) icing sugar

Heat the oven to 175°C (350°F). Grease a 30 × 23 cm (13 × 9 in.) rectangular baking pan.

Mix the soup and bicarbonate of soda in a bowl and set aside.

Cream the sugar, eggs, butter, spices and a pinch of salt. Add the soup. Sift the flour and baking powder and add to the mixture along with the raisins. Beat until well blended. Pour the batter into the baking dish.

Bake for 40 minutes or until a toothpick inserted in the centre comes out clean. Let the cake cool in the pan on a wire rack.

Beat the cream cheese, milk and vanilla extract until creamy. Slowly sift in the icing sugar until the icing is a suitable consistency to frost the cake.

Homage to Pablo Neruda's 'Ode to Tomatoes' (1954): Tomatoes Stuffed with Tuna

The Chilean poet Neruda wrote many odes to everyday food items such as tuna, lemons, pearly onions, jade-green artichokes and crimson tomatoes, using these items to encapsulate the human experience and make the ordinary extraordinary.

2 large, ripe beefsteak tomatoes
½ red onion, finely chopped
1 can tuna (200 g / 1 cup) in olive oil,
drained and flaked
½ celery stick, finely chopped
½ tbsp flat leaf parsley, finely chopped
1 tbsp lemon juice
2 tbsp mayonnaise
1 tbsp Dijon mustard
olive oil

salt and pepper
Parmesan, grated

Preheat the oven to 200°C (400°F).

Cut the top of the tomatoes and scoop out the seeds and juices, reserving some of the latter. Place the tomato halves upside down on a plate to drain further.

Fry the onion in a little olive oil until translucent, about five minutes. Set aside to cool then mix with the tuna, celery, parsley, lemon juice and enough reserved tomato seeds and juice to moisten.

Add the mayonnaise and mustard and season with salt and pepper.

Fill each tomato half with the tuna mixture and sprinkle with Parmesan. Place on a baking tray and bake for fifteen minutes.
Serves 4

Man-winning Tomato Salad (1951)

This famous salad was devised for a Wesson Oil promotion, a brand of cottonseed oil that was invented in 1889 in Memphis, Tennessee.

Cut six red-ripe tomatoes into wedges or slices. Top with one mild onion, chopped parsley to taste, and two tablespoons capers (optional). Your dressing is one-minute quick, and you can vary it so easily. So even this simple tomato salad has new surprise-flavor every day.

Wesson's One-minute French Dressing
½ tsp salt
¼ tsp sugar
⅛ tsp pepper
⅛ tsp paprika
⅓ cup Wesson Oil
2 tbsp vinegar or lemon juice

Shake together in a covered jar. Shake again before serving.
Makes ½ cup dressing

Easy-do Variations:
Celery Seed Dressing: To ½ cup of Wesson Dressing add 2 tsp sugar, ¼ tsp celery seed, and 1 tbsp catsup. Rub 4 butter-type crackers with garlic and crumble into dressing (for fruit or green salads, too).

Chili Dressing: To ½ cup of Wesson Dressing, add ½ tsp sugar, 2 tbsp chili sauce (for greens, meat or seafood salads).

California Avocado Open-face Sandwich (1974)

Under the strap-line 'The odd couple is a hot success', the following advertisement-cum-recipe described the sandwich as 'this year's sleeper'. In their marketing words, the mellow, nutlike flavour of the California avocado gets together with the honest texture of Ore-Ida shredded hash brown potatoes to make a sandwich 'something rather sensational'.

1 package Ore-Ida Shredded Hash Browns
1 large ripe California avocado, peeled and sliced
4 slices of American or Cheddar cheese, shredded
3 tbsp oil
salt and pepper
1 large or 2 small tomatoes

Heat oil in skillet; add hash browns. Fry until brown, turning carefully. Salt and pepper. Remove from skillet and place on broiler pan. Make layers of tomato and avocado strips on each patty. Top with cheese. Place under broiler for three to four minutes, until cheese melts. Cut patties in half. Serve hot.
Serves 4

Fried Green Tomatoes

Although seen as an iconic Southern classic, according to food historian Robert Moss, fried green tomatoes may well have entered the American culinary scene in the Northeast and Midwest in the late nineteenth century – well before their namesake movie put them on the global map.[3] This recipe, however, is an Italian version.

Some green tomatoes are meant to stay green forever, even when ripe. Others are unripe versions of red tomatoes that will eventually turn red. The latter can also be eaten while green and have a zingy, tart taste. This recipe can be made with either: the main requirement is that the texture be firm.

6 large green tomatoes
125 g (1 cup) plain flour
4 eggs
90 ml (⅓ cup) beer
300 g (3 cups) dried breadcrumbs
500 ml (2¼ cups) olive oil for frying
salt

Beat the eggs with the beer and pour into a shallow dish. Place the flour and breadcrumbs in two other dishes.

Cut the tomatoes into slices about 1 cm (approx. ½ inch) thick and blot with kitchen paper. Dip each slice into the flour, then into the beaten egg and finally the breadcrumbs. Dip each slice once more into the egg and breadcrumbs.

Heat the oil and fry several slices a time, cooking them for about ten minutes. Drain on kitchen paper and salt. Remove any batter residue from the oil before frying the next batch. Serve hot.
Serves 4–6

The Vroeman Family's
One and Only Dutch Tomato Soup

The Dutch and tomato soup go together like tulips and Amsterdam. Every family has their own recipe but as this belongs to mine, originating with the late John Vroeman, I claim it as the definitive version. It is also a good recipe for restoring the once-maligned reputation of the Dutch greenhouse tomato.

1.5 kg (3 lb 5 oz) tomatoes
1 leek, sliced
1 (winter) carrot, sliced
2 big or 3 small onions
1 potato (peeled and chopped into small pieces)
2 garlic cloves, finely chopped
2 bay leaves
crushed peppercorns
a 'sniff' of thyme
1 can tomato purée (100g / ⅓ cup)
40 g (3 tbsp) butter or margarine
water and beef stock (as much as seems right)
a piece of smoked bacon (100 g / ¾ cup)
250 g (1 cup) minced beef to make little balls for the soup (with
1 beaten egg, enough breadcrumbs to hold the mixture together,
thyme and oregano, and salt and pepper to taste)
plus a lot of patience and love

Immerse the tomatoes in boiling water for 30 seconds, then peel off the skin. Cut them into small pieces.

Cut 1 large or 2 small onions into small pieces. Set the remaining onion aside.

Melt most of the butter in a big pot and add the leek, carrot, chopped onions and garlic. Stir for five minutes to glaze them before adding the bay leaves, peppercorns and thyme plus the tomato purée.

Cook for several minutes, then add the tomatoes and potato. Cook gently until everything softens to the point of falling apart.

Blend all the ingredients or pass through a sieve. Put everything back in the pot with some water and beef stock, as much as seems appropriate (if you like a fairly thick soup, don't put in too much, you can always add more in the end).

Finely chop the remaining onion, as well as the bacon, and fry them until crispy in the rest of the butter. Add to the soup.

Make tiny meatballs (about a 1 cm or ½ in. in diameter), fry gently in butter and add to the soup.

It is ready to serve but, to be honest: the soup tastes much better the day after it is made.

Serves 4

Tomates à la Lucie (2007)
Joseph Delteil, *La Cuisine paléolithique* (Chartres, 2007), author's translation

The most beautiful tomato recipe in the world.

Take some perfectly round tomatoes, peel them and put in a pan to stew over a modest heat. Cook partially, neither too much nor too little, that is the art of it: the core of the tomato must stay raw, in its rust-brown skin. Cheeks on fire while the heart stays cool. Finally, sprinkle with plenty of chopped parsley and garlic. Serve with the juices poured over them. It puts me in mind of Scheherazade.

Killing Your Tomato

I was once asked by an Italian tomato grower why the British always 'murder' their tomatoes. Scene-of-the-crime, red-splattered visions aside, it emerged he was referring to the widespread habit of keeping tomatoes in the fridge. 'You buy a tomato, you eat it,' was his tomato world outlook, but he had a point. Variety, cultivation, season and storage conditions aside, tomatoes and certain other fruits do lose their flavour if refrigerated, as this turns off the enzyme system that helps produce fresh aroma and flavour. On the other hand, very ripe, fresh tomatoes may need to be refrigerated to stop them rotting. A fascinating, in-depth report by *Serious Eats* came to the conclusion that refrigeration is far more harmful to lower-quality and underripe tomatoes than it is to top-quality, in-season, freshly picked ones.[4] Just don't keep half a tomato wrapped in film – unless you really hate the Italians.

References

Introduction

1 Mark Harvey, Stephen Quilley and Huw Beynon, *Exploring the Tomato: Transformations of Nature, Society and Economy* (Cheltenham, Glos., and Northampton, MA, 2002), p. 103.
2 William Pritchard and David Burch, *Agri-food Globalization in Perspective: International Restructuring in the Processing Tomato Industry* (Farnham, Surrey, 2003), p. 247.
3 Harvey, Quilley and Benyon, *Exploring the Tomato*, p. 103.

1 Origins

1 Mark Harvey, Stephen Quilley and Huw Beynon, *Exploring the Tomato: Transformations of Nature, Society and Economy* (Cheltenham, Glos., and Northampton, MA, 2002), p. 1.
2 Charles M. Rick, 'The Tomato', *Scientific American*, CCXXXIX/2 (August 1978).
3 The 'invention' of the cherry tomato has often been attributed to Israeli horticulturalists. This is disputable: what is clear, however, is that their research transformed the cherry tomato into a mass-market commodity in the 1980s.
4 Rachel Laudan, *Cuisine and Empire: Cooking in World History* (Berkeley and Los Angeles, CA, 2013), p. 28.

5 Andrew F. Smith, *The Tomato in America: Early History, Culture and Cookery* (Urbana and Chicago, IL, 2001), p. 15.

6 J. A. Jenkins, 'The Origin of the Cultivated Tomato', *Economic Botany*, 11/4 (1948), pp. 379–92.

7 Janet Long, 'Tomatoes', in *The Cambridge World History of Food*, ed. Kenneth F. Kiple and Kriemhild Coneè Ornelas (Cambridge, 2000), vol. 11, Part 9, p. 353.

8 Sophie D. Coe, *America's First Cuisines* (Austin, TX, 1994), p. 117.

9 Long, 'Tomatoes', p. 353.

10 Ibid., p. 354.

11 Ibid., p. 353.

12 Laudan, *Cuisine and Empire*, p. 199.

13 Rebecca Earle, *The Body of the Conquistador: Food, Race and the Colonial Experience in Spanish America, 1492–1700* (Cambridge, 2014), p. 146.

2 New World to Old World

1 J. E. Hernández Bermejo and A. Lora González, 'Processes and Causes of Marginalisation: The Introduction of American Flora in Spain', in *Neglected Crops: 1492 from a Different Perspective*, ed. J. E. Hernández Bermejo and J. León (Rome, 1994) p. 266. There is some speculation that early seeds were sent to the Austrian court where the Spanish Emperor spent much time. J. A. Jenkins, The Origin of the Cultivated Tomato', *Economic Botany*, 11/4 (1948), p. 383.

2 Hernández Bermejo and Lora González, 'Processes and Causes of Marginalisation', p. 267.

3 Rudolf Grewe, 'The Arrival of the Tomato in Spain and Italy: Early Recipes', *Journal of Gastronomy*, 111/2 (1987).

4 Janet Long, 'Tomatoes', in *The Cambridge World History of Food*, ed. Kenneth F. Kiple and Kriemhild Coneè Ornelas (Cambridge, 2000), vol. 11, Part 9, p. 355.

5 Carolyn A. Nadeau, *Food Matters: Alonso Quijano's Diet and the Discourse of Food in Early Modern Spain* (Toronto, 2016), p. 88.

6 Jeanne Allard, 'El Tomate: Un Largo Trayecto Hasta la Mesa', *Historia Caribe*, II/6 (2001), pp. 45–54.

7 Maríaluz López-Terrada, 'The History of the Arrival of the Tomato in Europe: An Initial Overview', www.traditom.eu/history, accessed 5 September 2017.

8 Allard, 'El Tomate', pp. 45–54.

9 Nadeau, *Food Matters*, p. 90.

10 Long, Tomatoes', p. 355.

11 Vicky Hayward, *New Art of Cookery: A Spanish Friar's Kitchen* (Lanham, MD, and London, 2017), p. 258.

12 Nadeau, *Food Matters*, p. 90.

13 López-Terrada, 'The History of the Arrival of the Tomato in Europe'.

14 George Allen McCue, 'The History of the Use of the Tomato: An Annotated Bibliography,' *Annals of the Missouri Botanical Garden*, XXXIX/4 (1952), p. 327.

15 Nadeau, *Food Matters*, p. 90.

16 López-Terrada, 'The History of the Arrival of the Tomato in Europe'.

17 Hayward, *New Art of Cookery*, p. 18.

3 The Italian Tomato

1 The botanist Edgar Anderson credited the Turks with the diffusion of tomatoes into the eastern Mediterranean in the sixteenth century. They would likely have become acquainted with the plants in Italian or Spanish ports and taken them to other countries, much as they did when they took chilli pepper into Hungary in 1526.

2 David Gentilcore, *Pomodoro! A History of the Tomato in Italy* (New York and Chichester, West Sussex, 2010), p. 1.

3 Gillian Riley, *The Oxford Companion to Italian Food* (Oxford, 2007), p. 530.

4 George Allen McCue, 'The History of the Use of the Tomato: An Annotated Bibliography,' *Annals of the Missouri Botanical Garden*, XXXIX/4 (1952), p. 295.

5 Gentilcore, *Pomodoro!*, p. 11.
6 Andrew F. Smith, *The Tomato in America: Early History, Culture, and Cookery* (Urbana and Chicago, IL, 2001), p. 21.
7 Gentilcore, *Pomodoro!*, p. 4.
8 Rudolf Grewe, 'The Arrival of the Tomato in Spain and Italy: Early Recipes', *Journal of Gastronomy*, III/2 (1987).
9 Ken Albala, *Food in Early Modern Europe* (Westport, CT, 2003), p. 32.
10 Fabio Parasecoli, *Al Dente: A History of Food in Italy* (London, 2014), p. 119.
11 Gentilcore, *Pomodoro!*, p. 48.
12 John Dickie, *Delizia!: The Epic History of the Italians and their Food* (London, 2007), p. 171.
13 Gentilcore, *Pomodoro!*, p. 57.
14 Ibid., p. 45.
15 Ibid., pp. 56–8.
16 Andrew F. Smith, *Souper Tomatoes: The Story of America's Favorite Food* (New Brunswick, NJ, and London, 2000), p. 27.
17 Piero Camporesi, *The Magic Harvest: Food, Folklore and Society* (Malden, MA, 1998), p. 127.
18 See www.museidelcibio.it, accessed 5 September 2017.
19 Gentilcore, *Pomodoro!*, p. 156.
20 Massimo Montanari, *Let the Meatballs Rest: And Other Stories About Food and Culture* (New York and Chichester, West Sussex, 2012), p. 112.
21 Camporesi, *Magic Harvest*, p. 128.
22 Ibid., p. 116.
23 Dave DeWitt, *Precious Cargo: How Foods from the Americas Changed the World* (Berkeley, CA, 2014), p. 174.
24 Arthur Allen, *Ripe: The Search for the Perfect Tomato* (Berkeley, CA, 2010), p. 179.

4 Elsewhere in Europe

1 Georges Gibault, *Histoire des légumes* (Chartres, 2015), p. 348.

2   Barbara Santich, 'A la recherche de la tomate perdue: The First French Tomato Recipe?', *Gastronomica*, II/2 (2002), pp. 68–71.

3   Evelyne Bloch-Dano, *Vegetables: A Biography* (Chicago, IL, and London, 2012), p. 73.

4   George Allen McCue, 'The History of the Use of the Tomato: An Annotated Bibliography', *Annals of the Missouri Botanical Garden*, XXXIX/4 (1952), pp. 313–14.

5   Ibid., p. 314.

6   Andrew F. Smith, *The Tomato in America: Early History, Culture and Cookery* (Urbana and Chicago, IL, 2001), p. 17.

7   Jonathan Roberts, *Cabbages and Kings: The Origins of Fruit and Vegetables* (London, 2001), p. 201.

8   Paul Freedman, ed., *Food: The History of Taste* (Berkeley and Los Angeles, CA, 2007), p. 213.

9   Kate Colquhoun, *Taste: The Story of Britain through its Cooking* (London, New York and Berlin, 2008), p. 266. Apparently Jane adored them, writing to ask her sister Cassandra whether she had any spare.

10 Smith, *The Tomato in America*, p. 20.

11 'Love-Apple, or Tomato Berry', *The Times* (London, 22 September 1820).

12 Christopher Stocks, *Forgotten Fruits: A Guide to Britain's Traditional Fruit and Vegetables* (London, 2008), p. 208.

13 Andrew F. Smith, *Souper Tomatoes: The Story of America's Favorite Food* (New Brunswick, NJ, and London, 2000), p. 49.

14 Mark Harvey, Stephen Quilley and Huw Beynon, *Exploring the Tomato: Transformations of Nature, Society and Economy* (Cheltenham, Glos., and Northampton, MA, 2002), p. 36.

15 David Gentilcore, *Pomodoro!: A History of the Tomato in Italy* (New York and Chichester, West Sussex, 2010), p. 26.

16 Stewart Lee Allen, *In the Devil's Garden: A Sinful History of Forbidden Food* (Edinburgh, 2003), p. 21.

17 Sophie Coe, *America's First Cuisines* (Austin, TX, 1999), p. 49.

18 In China, tomatoes have the properties of being sweet, sour and slightly cold and are believed to strengthen the stomach, promote digestion and cleanse the liver.

19 Reay Tannahill, *Food in History* (New York, 1973), p. 207.

20 Elisabeth Rozin, *The Primal Cheeseburger* (New York, 1994), p. 98. She also notes the existence of a village in Turkey whose inhabitants ate only underripe green tomatoes because the red ripe ones were considered too 'bloody'. By contrast, according to Evelyne Bloch-Dano in *Vegetables: A Biography* (p. 75), although tomato juice for the Bambara tribe of Mali symbolizes blood, it also represents menstrual blood and therefore fertility. Women offer tomatoes to the divinity, and couples eat a tomato before intercourse.

21 Eliezer Segal, *Ask Now of the Days that are Past* (Calgary, 2005), p. 266.

22 Joan Nathan, *Jewish Cooking in America* (New York, 1994), p. 239.

23 Ofra Tene, 'The New Immigrant Must Not only Learn, He Must Also Forget', *Jews and their Foodways*, ed. Anat Helman (New York, 2015), p. 53.

24 Quoted in Ofra Tene, 'The New Immigrant', p. 53.

5 Back to America

1 Mark Twain, *A Tramp Abroad* (Mineola, NY, 2002), p. 278.

2 Alfred W. Crosby, *The Columbian Exchange: Biological and Cultural Consequences of 1492* (Westport, CT, 2003), p. 64.

3 Waverley Root and Richard De Rochemont, *Eating in America: A History* (Hopewell, NJ, 1995), p. 54.

4 Ibid., p. 10.

5 Andrew F. Smith, *The Tomato in America: Early History, Culture, and Cookery* (Urbana and Chicago, IL, 2001), p. 42.

6 Andrew F. Smith, ed., *The Oxford Companion to American Food and Drink* (Oxford and New York, 2007), p. 335.

7 Smith, *The Tomato in America*, pp. 6–8.

8 Peter J. Hatch, *'A Rich Spot of Earth': Thomas Jefferson's Revolutionary Garden at Monticello* (New Haven, CT, and London, 2012), p. 157.

9 Smith, *The Tomato in America*, pp. 37–40.

10 Robert Buist, *The Family Kitchen Gardener* (Charleston, SC, 2008), pp. 125–6.

11 Smith, *The Tomato in America*, p. 41.

12 Megan J. Elias, *Food in the United States, 1890–1945* (Santa Barbara, CA, Denver, CO, and Oxford, 2009), p. 19.

13 Hasia R. Diner, *Hungering for America: Italian, Irish and Jewish Foodways in the Age of Migration* (Cambridge, MA, 2003), pp. 62–8.

14 Nicolò de Quattrociocchi, *Love and Dishes* (New York, 1950).

15 Smith, *Tomato in America*, p. 102.

16 Ibid., p. 133.

17 Ibid., p. 135.

18 Andrew F. Smith, *Souper Tomatoes: The Story of America's Favorite Food* (New Brunswick, NJ, and London, 2000), p. 37.

19 Alissa Overend, 'Cancer-fighting Foods', in *The SAGE Encyclopedia of Food Issues*, ed. Ken Albala (Thousand Oaks, London, New Delhi and Singapore, 2015), vol. 1, p. 164.

20 See www.mdpi.com, accessed 5 September 2017.

21 See www.sciencedaily.com/releases/2017/5, accessed 5 September 2017.

22 Susanne Grether-Beck et al., 'Molecular Evidence that Oral Supplementation with Lycopene or Lutein Protects Human Skin against Ultraviolet Radiation: Results from a Double-blind, Placebo-controlled, Crossover Study', *British Journal of Dermatology* (May 2017), CLXXVI/5.

23 Scott M. Ebert et al., 'Identification and Small Molecule Inhibition of an Activating Transcription Factor 4 (ATF4)-dependent Pathway to Age-related Skeletal Muscle Weakness and Atrophy', *Journal of Biological Chemistry*, CCXC/37 (15 October 2015), pp. 25497–551.

24 Andrew F. Smith, *Pure Ketchup: A History of America's National Condiment* (Columbia, SC, 1996), p. 140.

6 Soup and Ketchup

1 Much information in this chapter derives from *Souper Tomatoes: The Story of America's Favorite Food* (New Brunswick, NJ, and London, 2000) and *Pure Ketchup: A History of America's National Condiment* (Columbia, SC, 1996), both by Andrew F. Smith.

2 Waverley Root and Richard De Rochemont, *Eating in America: A History* (Hopewell, NJ, 1995), p. 190.

3 Susan Williams, *Food in the United States, 1820s–1890* (Westport, CT, 2006), p. 79.

4 Smith, *Souper Tomatoes*, p. 22.

5 Mark Harvey, Stephen Quilley and Huw Beynon, *Exploring the Tomato: Transformations of Nature, Society and Economy* (Cheltenham, Glos., and Northampton, MA, 2002), p. 4.

6 Harvey Levenstein, *Revolution at the Table: The Transformation of the American Diet* (Berkeley and Los Angeles, CA, and London, 2003), p. 168.

7 Elisabeth Rozin, *The Primal Cheeseburger* (New York and London, 1994), p. 101.

8 Ibid., p. 103.

9 Smith, *Pure Ketchup*, p. 43.

7 Glasshouses and Beyond

1 Mark Harvey, Stephen Quilley and Huw Beynon, *Exploring the Tomato: Transformations of Nature, Society and Economy* (Cheltenham, Glos., and Northampton, MA, 2002), p. 38.

2 John Hoenig, 'A Tomato for All Seasons: Innovation in American Agricultural Production, 1900–1945', *Harvard Business History Review*, LXXXVII/3 (Autumn 2014), pp. 523–44.

3 Ibid.

4 Ibid.

5 Harvey, Quilley and Beynon, *Exploring the Tomato*, p. 84. After complaints, the Dutch 'invented' cluster tomatoes (attached to the vine) to show how ripe their fruit was.

6 Ibid., p. 102.

7 See www.britishtomatoes.co.uk/environment, accessed 5 September 2017.

8 'Tomatoes: Trends Towards 2020', paper given at the Tomato Conference 2016 (Antwerp, Belgium).

9 See www.arizona.edu/hydroponictomatoes, accessed 5 September 2017.

10 Bernard Dichek, 'Salad Bowl for the Desert', *Jerusalem Report* (22 August 2016).

11 Leah Simpson, 'How This City is Developing a Farm in the Heart of the Desert', www.theculturetrip.com, 26 September 2018.

12 Lorena Galliot, 'July 4 Barbecues Welcome Infrared Tomatoes and Meatless Meat', *The Daily Climate*, 4 July 2014.

13 See www.french-news-online.com, 19 April 2015.

14 See www.freshplaza.com, 28 September 2016.

15 Andrew F. Smith, *Souper Tomatoes: The Story of America's Favorite Food* (New Brunswick, NJ, and London, 2000), p. 58.

16 Hoenig, 'A Tomato for All Seasons', pp. 523–44.

17 Arthur Allen, *Ripe: The Search for the Perfect Tomato* (Berkeley, CA, 2010), p. 82; Harvey, Quilley and Beynon, *Exploring the Tomato*, p. 12.

18 Evan D. G. Fraser and Andrew Rimas, *Empires of Food: Feast, Famine, and the Rise and Fall of Civilizations* (New York and London, 2010), p. 156.

19 Hoenig, 'A Tomato for All Seasons', pp. 523–44.

20 'New Tomato Harvest Robot GROW being Tested in the Greenhouse', www.freshplaza.com, 20 June 2018.

21 Barry Estabrook, 'Chemical Warfare', in *Tomatoland: How Modern Industrial Agriculture Destroyed Our Most Alluring Fruit* (Kansas City, MO, 2012), pp. 35–72.

22 Estabrook, 'A Penny Per Pound', in *Tomatoland*, pp. 121–38.

23 'U.S. Tomato Farm Workers March against Wendy's Fast Food Chain', www.freshplaza.com, 14 May 2018.

24 See www.telesurtv.net/english/news/Italy, 29 March 2016.
25 Jane Moyo, 'Abdou, a Migrant Worker, Picks Italian
    Tomatoes but Barely Earns a Living', www.ethicaltrade.org,
    18 December 2015; Andrew Weasley, 'Scandal of the
    "Tomato Slaves" Harvesting Crop Exported to the UK',
    www.theecologist.org, 1 September 2011.

8 Varieties, Organics and Heirlooms

1   Andrew F. Smith, *The Tomato in America: Early History, Culture,
    and Cookery* (Urbana and Chicago, IL, 2011), pp. 16–17.
2   Ibid., p. 64.
3   Craig LeHoullier, *Epic Tomatoes: How to Select and Grow the Best
    Varieties of All Time* (North Adams, MA, 2015), p. 26.
4   Ibid., p. 43.
5   Ibid., p. 100.
6   Report by the author from Tomato Conference 2016
    (Antwerp, Belgium).
7   See 'Tomatoes That Don't Rot Discovered in France',
    www.freshplaza.com, 7 October 2014.
8   See 'Abundant to Take Extreme Veggies to Market',
    www.sbs.com.au, 7 April 2016.
9   Dave DeWitt, *Precious Cargo: How Foods from the Americas
    Changed the World* (Berkeley, CA, 2014), pp. 339–41.
10 See www.ewg.org/foodnews/dirty_dozen_list, accessed
    5 September 2017.
11 Barry Estabrook, *Tomatoland: How Modern Industrial
    Agriculture Destroyed Our Most Alluring Fruit* (Kansas City,
    MO, 2012), pp. 20 and 41.
12 Joanna Wood, 'Protecting UK Tomatoes the Natural Way',
    www.fruitnet.com, 3 April 2017.
13 Tim Stark, *Heirloom: Notes From an Accidental Tomato Farmer*
    (New York, 2008), p. 63.
14 See www.aerogarden.com, accessed 5 September 2017.
15 'Tomatoes for Hanging, the True Flavour of Spanish
    Cuisine', www.freshplaza.com, 21 August 2017. The famous

sweet and crunchy Raf, born in Marmande in France and raised in Almerian red soil and saline water, is protected by a European PGI.

16 Michele Anna Jordan, *The Good Cook's Book of Tomatoes* (New York, 2015), pp. 28–9.

17 Jennifer A. Jordan, *Edible Memory: The Lure of Heirloom Tomatoes and Other Forgotten Foods* (Chicago, IL, and London, 2015), p. 54.

18 Christopher Stocks, *Forgotten Fruits: A Guide to Britain's Traditional Fruit and Vegetables* (London, 2008), pp. 206–12.

19 'TX2022 tomatoes from Meridiem Seeds', www.freshplaza. com, 4 April 2017.

9 Science and Technology

1 Mark Harvey, Stephen Quilley and Huw Beynon, *Exploring the Tomato: Transformations of Nature, Society and Economy* (Cheltenham, Glos., and Northampton, MA, 2002), p. 129.

2 See www.norfolkplantsciences.com, accessed 5 September 2017.

3 Ferris Jabr, 'Reclaiming the Lost Flavor of Heirloom Produce: Without GMOs', *Scientific American* (June 2015).

4 Edward Hammond, 'Aided by Genomic Technologies, the Patent Pillage of Andean Tomato Diversity Continues', *Biopiracy Watch Briefing*, Third World Network Info Service on Biodiversity and Traditional Knowledge, 5 May 2015.

5 Jabr, 'Reclaiming the Lost Flavor', *Scientific American*.

6 Hammond, 'Aided by Genomic Technologies'; see also '65,000 × Opposition Against Syngenta Patent on Tomatoes', www.seedfreedom.info, 12 May 2016.

7 Aaron I. Velez-Ramirez et al., 'A Single Locus Confers Tolerance to Continuous Light and Allows Substantial Yield Increase in Tomato', www.nature.com, 5 August 2014.

8 'Technology Institute Devlops Tomato which becomes More Tasty Under Stress', www.freshplaza.com, 22 August 2018.

9 American Chemical Society, 'Generating Electricity with
   Tomato Waste', www.acs.org, 16 March 2016.
10 Pilar Rojas-Gracia et al., 'The Parthenocarpic *Hydra* Mutant
   Reveals a New Function for a SPOROCYTELESS-like Gene in
   the Control of Fruit Set in Tomato', *New Phytologist*, CCXIV/3
   (May 2017), pp. 1198–12.
11 Corinne Iozzio, 'Making Car Parts from Tomatoes',
   www.smithsonianmag.com, 18 June 2014.
12 'Spain: Discovery of Key Gene in the Production of
   Seedless Tomatoes', www.freshplaza.com, 21 April 2018.
13 'Cardboard Made from Tomato Plants Wins European
   Sustainability Prize', www.freshplaza.com, 1 September
   2016.
14 'Trays Made from Recycled Tomato Plant Fibres',
   www.freshplaza.com, 11 January 2017.
15 'Tomatoes for Cosmetics', www.bbrsc.ac.uk, 4 August 2014.
16 Elizabeth Howell, 'Antarctica Greenhouse Produces
   Cucumbers, Tomatoes and More in Mars-like Test',
   www.space.com, 24 September 2018.
17 'A Satellite Goes on a Journey – with Tomatoes on Board',
   www.dlr.de/dlr/en, 18 October 2018.

Recipes

1 Andrew F. Smith, *The Tomato in America, Early History,
   Culture, and Cookery* (Urbana and Chicago, IL, 2001), p. 74.
2 Christopher Stocks, *Forgotten Fruits: A Guide to Britain's
   Traditional Fruit and Vegetables* (London, 2008), pp. 207–8.
3 Robert Moss, 'The Hollywood Effect: How Fried Green
   Tomatoes became a Southern "Classic"', www.seriouseats.
   com, October 2014.
4 Daniel Gritzer, 'How to Store Tomatoes (and Whether to
   Refrigerate) Them', www.seriouseats.com, September 2014.

Select Bibliography

Allen, Arthur, *Ripe: The Search for the Perfect Tomato* (Berkeley, CA, 2010)

Estabrook, Barry, *Tomatoland: How Modern Industrial Agriculture Destroyed Our Most Alluring Fruit* (Kansas City, MO, 2012)

Gentilcore, David, *Pomodoro! A History of the Tomato in Italy* (New York and Chichester, 2010)

Harvey, Mark, Stephen Quilley and Huw Beynon, *Exploring the Tomato: Transformations of Nature, Society and Economy* (Cheltenham, Glos., and Northampton, MA, 2002)

Jordan, Jennifer A., *Edible Memory: The Lure of Heirloom Tomatoes and Other Forgotten Foods* (Chicago, IL, and London, 2015)

LeHoullier, Craig, *Epic Tomatoes: How to Select and Grow the Best Varieties of All Time* (North Adams, MA, 2015)

Smith, Andrew F., *Pure Ketchup: A History of America's National Condiment* (Columbia, SC, 2012)

—, *Souper Tomatoes: The Story of America's Favorite Food* (New Brunswick, NJ, and London, 2000)

—, *The Tomato in America: Early History, Culture, and Cookery* (Urbana and Chicago, IL, 2001)

Websites and Associations

British Tomato Growers' Association
www.britishtomatoes.co.uk

California Tomato Growers Association
www.ctga.org

Florida Tomatoes
www.floridatomatoes.org

Seed Savers Exchange
www.seedsavers.org

Tatiana's TOMATObase
www.tatianastomatobase.com

Tomato Genetics Resource Center, UC Davis
www.tgrc.ucdavis.edu

Traditom
www.traditom.eu

Acknowledgements

Many thanks to Andrew F. Smith for initial guidance and his willingness to allow me to plunder his extensive research.

Photo Acknowledgements

The author and publishers wish to express their thanks to the below sources of illustrative material and/or permission to reproduce it.

Reproduced courtesy the Agricultural Research Service (United States Department of Agriculture): p. 8; photo © Ariadna126/ iStock International Inc.: p. 22; from Giorgio Bonelli, *Hortus Romanus juxta systema Tournefortianum Paulo* . . . (photo courtesy New York Public Library – Rare Book Division): p. 36; from *The Boston Cooking-School Magazine*, XIII/3 (October 1896): p. 83; photo © BrilliantEye/iStock International Inc.: p. 79; photo Robert Brook/Alamy Stock Photo: p. 115; photo Dorotheum: p. 33; from *The Florists' Review*, XLVII/1216 (17 March 1921): p. 88; photo Fructibus: p. 28; photo © Gorodenkoff/iStock International Inc.: p. 121; photo Gzzzz: p. 26; photo © ilbusca/iStock International Inc.: p. 48; from the *Johnson & Stokes Garden & Farm Manual* (Philadelphia, PA, 1890): p. 112; from *The Ladies' Home Journal*, LXIV/1 (January 1947): p. 70; photos Library of Congress Washington, DC, Prints and Photographs Division: pp. 72 (National Child Labor Collection), 74; photo Mary Evans Picture Library: p. 37; photo Mary Evans Picture Library/Retrograph Collection: p. 49; from Matthäus Merian, *Hispalis vulgo Sevilliæ urbis toto orbe celeberrimæ primaria effigies Hispaniæque* (Amsterdam, 1638): p. 26; Metropolitan Museum of Art (Open Access): p. 62; from *Moore and Simon's Seed Buyers Guide and Wholesale Price List* (Philadelphia, PA, 1902): p. 86;

photo mycola/Istock International Inc.: p. 12; photo courtesy the National Agricultural Library (United States Department of Agriculture) – Henry G. Gilbert Nursery and Seed Trade Catalog Collection: p. 10; photo courtesy The National Library of Medicine, Bethesda, Maryland: p. 51; from *Le Petit Journal*, no. 504 (15 July 1900): p. 37; private collections: pp. 27, 33; from James Smiley, *Smiley's Cook Book and Universal Household Guide* (Chicago, IL, 1895): p. 52; from Karl Stieler, *Italy from the Alps to Mount Etna* (London, 1877): p. 38; United States Department of the Treasury (Office of War Information), reproduced courtesy of the National Archives and Records Administration: pp. 64, 75.

jeffreyw has published the image on p. 44, Jeremy Keith the image on p. 9 and Jeremy Thompson the images on pp. 67 and 70, under conditions imposed by a Creative Commons Attribution 2.0 Generic license; Andy Melton has published the image on p. 60, chipmunk_1 the images on pp. 10 and 11, cyclonebill the images on pp. 29 and 43, flydime the image on p. 13 and Lula Farms the image on p. 93, under conditions imposed by a Creative Commons Attribution-Share Alike 2.0 Generic license; KENPEI has published the image on p. 16 under conditions imposed by a Creative Commons Attribution-Share Alike 2.1 Japan license; Vmenkov has published the image on p. 105 under conditions imposed by Creative Commons Attribution-Share Alike 3.0 Unported, 2.5 Generic, 2.0 Generic and 1.0 Generic licenses; Assianir has published the image on p. 111, Coentor has published the image on p. 17, Guilhem Vellut the image on p. 84, Ji-Elle the image on p. 39, Leitatosaichong the image on p. 14, Marisa Pérez the image on p. 63, the Musei del Cibo della Provincia di Parma the image on p. 41, MyAeroponics the image on p. 91, Oppidum Nissenae the image on p. 82, Sharon Gefen the image on p. 58, and Six Sigma the image on p. 78, under conditions imposed by a Creative Commons Attribution-Share Alike 3.0 Unported license; Samuel C Kessler has published the image on p. 92 under conditions imposed by a Creative Commons Attribution 4.0 International license; David Adam Kess has published the image on p. 100, Kjerish the image on p. 27, Schumi4ever the image on p. 90, Sixflashphoto the image on p. 102, and Varaine the image on p. 46, under conditions imposed by a Creative Commons Attribution-Share Alike 4.0 International license. Readers are free to share – to copy, distribute and transmit this image alone; or to remix – to adapt this image alone, under the following conditions: attribution – readers must attribute the image in the manner specified by the author or licensor (but not in any way that suggests that these parties endorse them or their use of the work).

Index

italic numbers refer to illustrations; **bold** to recipes